STEADFAST AWARENESS:
REFLECTIONS AND LIFE'S TAKEAWAYS

BY
MATTHEW EDMUND AIREY

Legal Notices:

Copyright © 2020 The Airey Revocable Living Trust – March 13, 2017

All rights reserved. No part of this website content may be reproduced in any form or by any means without written consent of Matthew Edmund Airey or The Airey Revocable Living Trust – March 13, 2017 (the publisher) except as provided by the United States copyright law or in the case of brief quotes used in published articles and reviews.

The scanning, uploading, and distribution of this website content via the internet or via any other means without the permission of Matthew Edmund Airey or The Airey Revocable Living Trust – March 13, 2017 (the publisher) is illegal and punishable by law.

Matthew Edmund Airey,

The Airey Revocable Living Trust – March 13, 2017, and

MA Consulting (MAC).

Chino Hills, CA 91709

https://www.linkedin.com/in/matthewairey/

mattairey.com

Please go to Amazon.com or other online retailers to purchase this book or an electronic or Kindle version of this book. Thank you.

ISBN: 9798670988834

About the Book:

Through decades of professional experience in technology, finance, and consulting, Matthew Edmund Airey navigated through personal and professional loss of life. Steadfast Awareness and perseverance define his outlook. In his reflections, Airey offers joyous memories of his loved ones, their deaths, and moving forward. He believes confronting challenges is the only way to overcome them. Each chapter invites personal reflection with question prompts to direct focus to the present. The author hopes the book will guide readers to find meaning in their own tragedies and cherished memories in Life's Takeaways.

Airey is the son of two California schoolteachers and worked as an adolescent on his family ranch. Some of his reflections were cultivated during his high school years. Airey says being present, listening to, and caring about people you encounter is the best way to forge meaningful relationships. He includes personal poems to his mother and friends to express himself, and encourages the reader to do the same. Airey shares 18 business reflections that directly influenced his consulting and personal strategies. His work and life's contests forced him to fundamentally appreciate his immigrant ancestors, close family and friends. He believes engaging our shared humanity could be a powerful antidote to contemporary American social ills. In the text he advocates for a Steadfast Awareness — to refocus on those people and values that matter most.

ABOUT THE AUTHOR:

Matthew Edmund Airey's work and consulting leadership experience encompasses over 30 years of technology, operations, and finance knowledge. He holds a Master of Business Administration Degree from Loyola Marymount University in Los Angeles, California. Airey also holds Bachelor of Arts Degrees in Public Relations Journalism and Communication Arts and Sciences from the University of Southern California in Los Angeles, California. He enjoys traveling and volunteering and is a member of the United States Coast Guard Auxiliary. Airey resides in Chino Hills, California with his family.

Matthew is available for consulting contracts and speaking engagements via the contact information provided.

Matthew Airey
MA Consulting (MAC)
Chino Hills, CA 91709
https://www.linkedin.com/in/matthewairey/
mattairey.com

Please go to Amazon.com or other online retailers to purchase this book or an electronic or Kindle version of this book. Thank you.

Steadfast Awareness:
Reflections and Life's Takeaways

by **Matthew Edmund Airey**

Dedication:

To my beautiful wife, Christy Ann Airey.

To my sons:
Garrett Matthew Airey
Shane Abbott Airey
Connor James Airey

To my grandchildren and to my great grandchildren, whom I have yet to see face-to-face or whom I will see from afar.

I hope you all come to know how deeply I love you.
Care for you. Proud of you.

Contents

PROLOGUE: Gratitude... 1

Chapter 1: "I Wrote a Book. So What?".. 4

Chapter 2: Cold Tears... 10

Chapter 3: "We Only Make It Complex."..................................... 16

Chapter 4: "A Tree, A Team, and A Testimony"......................... 31

Chapter 5: "Quiet Heart".. 36

Chapter 6: "Gratitude. Formation. Legacy."............................... 39

Chapter 7: "I'm The Quarterback."... 56

Chapter 8: "Mike liked Brunettes. I liked Blonds."................... 74

Chapter 9. My Best Friend's Wedding. "With Me, Free Me."..... 78

Chapter 10: "From Far, Far Away"... 81

Chapter 11: "Aunt Kathy, You're Not Singing Loud Enough!"..... 84

Chapter 12: "That's My Nephew, Matthew."............................. 88

Chapter 13: "God Doesn't Have A Watch."................................ 94

Chapter 14: "Who has the X on their forehead?"
Business Reflections... 99

Chapter 15: "Nana, Where's My Microphone?"......................117

Chapter 16: Maintain Steadfast Awareness
and Realize Your Life's Takeaways..127

Appendix A: In Loving Memory of Edmund Francis Airey, Jr.
June 27, 1928 – November 4, 2001. 131

Appendix B: In Loving Memory of Marguerite June Airey.
June 4, 1933 – January 6, 2020..134

Appendix C: In Memory of US Navy Commander
William Joseph "Bill" Gault. 1954 - 2019..................................138

PROLOGUE: Gratitude

I am eternally grateful for my great-great grandparents and my-great-grandparents, who immigrated to the United States of America.

The only reason I am here is because someone decided to get on a boat.

President John F. Kennedy said it best,

> "When my great-grandfather left here to become a cooper in East Boston, he carried nothing with him except two things - a strong religious faith and a strong desire for liberty."
> — No Irish Need Apply.

This was such the case of my ancestors and that of most Americans.

We Americans need to continue to pray for peace and work for justice for all of our citizens; and for the citizens of the world.

I am grateful for my parents, Edmund Francis Airey, Jr. and Marguerite June (Gerberick) Airey.

Dad, Daddy, Dada, Eddie, Junior, Edmundo Segundo, Monk, Chet, Tex, and Papa to his grandchildren: For your strong faith, hard work, humor and laughter, and duty to others, and encouraging letters and cards.

Mom, Ma, Mama, Rittie Rite, Aunt Rite, Margo, Maggie, Marg, and Nana to her grandchildren: For your creativeness, love of country and history, quick wit, and compassion for all. For your love and prayers.

And for my sister, Regina Marie Airey. For listening, for caring, and for timeless support to my parents and my family and me. Her critical thinking and strategic entrepreneurship are exemplary.

Don and Janelle Denison. Joe Frazzette. For their publishing guidance and encouragement.

James Joseph Duffy V, my Godson. For his patience and editing skills.

My godmother, Adrienne Maureen (Airey) Larsen. My godfather, Michael Engh, S.J.

My godchildren: Joanna Airey, Trisha Engh, James Joseph Duffy V, Justin Abbott, Ryan Arellano, Caitlyn Busso Welch, Patrick Baiza, Debbie Burns, and Nash Matthew Maywood.

My confirmation candidates: Rafael Ojeda, Danny Ojeda, Victor Ojeda, Sean Keating, and Alex Munoz.

My in-laws, nieces, nephews, and their extended families: Abbotts, Baizas, Culps, and Klines.

My nephew, Cody Robert Culp. March 21, 1989 – January 14, 2020. Cody did not say much, but when he did, it counted. "Do Work" was the phrase he used to encourage his older brother, James, to complete college and continue to move forward productively with his life. "Too much drama" was Cody's comical commentary on overly emotional relationships or issues that became too personal. He would rather enjoy good company with family and friends, than manage drama.

I am eternally indebted to my teachers, coaches, religious order priests, sisters and nuns, and my classmates who showed me tolerance, compassion, and support through all my years.

In particular those from:

Saint Martha Catholic School, La Puente, California.

Bishop Amat Memorial High School, La Puente, CA. Go Lancers! Steadfast, Loyal, and True.

University of Southern California, Los Angeles, CA. Fight On!

Loyola Marymount University Master of Business Administration (MBA) program, Los Angeles, CA (and prerequisite graduate work at San Diego State University).

I am grateful to all of my work colleagues, managers, and clients and to my personal attorneys. Through the years you have inspired me to be a better person and a better leader and to strive for desired results, while being very personal, strategic and tactical.

####

As my father drove me to school in the morning, we would say this prayer together out loud. We would next give each other a kiss, and then start our day — what a lifelong foundation in which to thrive and to strive.

Good Morning Sweet Jesus.
I love you and adore you.
Watch over me this day and always.
God Bless Dad, Mom, ____, ____ (name family members here).
And All of Our Fighting Men, and bring all wars and evil to a quick end.
And help us to do our best in everything.
Amen.

Postscript: The Fighting Men reference represented the American Troops during the Vietnam War Era (And All U.S. Veterans).

Chapter 1: "I Wrote a Book. So What?"

The inspiration for this book has been gathered and is not limited to these book chapters of a lifetime of experiences and thoughts. It originated during my years at Bishop Amat Memorial High School, in La Puente, California from 1976 through 1980. You must remember this was a time before cell phones, the Internet, instant news, and instant communication. Modes of entertainment were the movies, the radio, and LPs. And maybe some cassette players, and for sure maybe some 8-track tape players at that time.

As young a teenager in the 1970s, you still had to personally talk to people; you were physically face to face with them. You still had to go out of your way to meet them, to be engaged as friends, as a couple or a group of friends or as a team. Some of my best friends at the time and still today were James "Jimmy" Joseph Duffy IV and Enrique "Call Me Hank" Arellano. Man, am I lucky to be blessed with so many dear close and caring friends. Since we had limited money and somewhat unlimited time, and we came from very humble beginnings, we had to find ways to entertain ourselves and each other without spending money (or getting into much trouble with the law).

So, my two friends and I came up with an imaginative manner of which to amuse ourselves and pass the time we had in our youth. We would try to spin stories, create characters, and perform imitations of people that we knew of with the purpose of just trying to see who could get the first laugh, the last laugh, or any kind of a courtesy laugh. We would announce imaginary football games with English and Spanish commentaries within the field announcer's booth that we would sneak into. Our imaginations supported each other and built our confidence to face an unsure world after our high school years.

On one of our inspired occasions of banter, my friend Jimmy started to imagine himself as a fictional character, who had everything in life going against him. No money, little talent, poor economic factors, and the charter that he had to live his life "fighting the current." What an incredible concept. The challenging possibilities facing the character could be endless. Each one of us took turns on how our character interacted within arduous environments, such as ocean rip currents on SoCal beaches, and how he would fight the current. So much fun and laughter and engagement between frivol less young, close friends.

This is the origin for this book, since I never forgot about this inventive concept. So, I pretty much stole it from Jimmy. (What a good buddy I am? Good buddies don't ask, they just take. Another inside stupid saying we came up with.). But please note that all of the content copyrights now belong to me, ha ha. That was a pretty good take by me, especially since Jimmy is now an attorney.

However, I realized after I completed the book's chapters, that I needed to edit the title. Fighting the current was somewhat of a basic and overused title. It is relative to my teenage antics, but the book's content required better representation. Thus, I chose <u>Steadfast Awareness</u> as the book's title to advocate for being present in the moment. The title my youthful high school attentiveness of my history and potential future. Chapter 16 articulates key references to my steadfast awareness. But my steadfast awareness, and hopefully yours, continued through my youth until today. I added the subtitle <u>Reflections and Life's Takeaways</u> to simply note that this book contains my memories and experiences. Yet, life's takeaways imply losing a loved one, but more importantly, what lessons were learned and the conclusions the reader takes from their own challenges and joys.

Note: Below content similar to before.

The "'so what?'" response of my book's submission is indicative of going against social and emotional norms. I am not an anarchist or radical, but I advocate that a person has to set their own path in life guided by a sound moral compass. That is why the stories and emotions in this book are the most meaningful to me. However, I really don't care if they are meaningful to the reader or other people, I just wanted to share my reflections and make people really think and contemplate about **_their own lives and their current circumstances_**. So what? This refers to being present, while reflecting on "the currents" that are now flowing or have flowed through your life experience, not necessarily mine.

I found that sometimes you have to do things in a unique way, think of things in a unique way, and say things in a unique way to be successful or to get the results that you need. As well as being unique to really collaborate and get along with others towards a common and achievable goal. So, Steadfast Awareness contains numerous personal reflections (and some business insights) that I am passionate about. However, their individualities are truly intended as only catalysts to reflect, discover, and document how they are meaningfully applicable in your (unique) life (the reader's).

I decided to write down my thoughts and experiences, not to be self-serving. But I do like to write, and I do like to share thoughts, ideas, and experiences that I find may have some commonality with others. This book was written for and dedicated to my wife, my sons, my grandchildren, and my great grandchildren.

Why? Our current society has a more and more difficult time of communicating with one another. Although technology is a fantastic medium and should be celebrated, I really don't think it replaces the permanency of the written word and more so the pertinence of one on one communication or one to group communications that we experience in our day-to-day lives at work and with family and friends. I also find now that many times, and this is not a direct criticism of my family or friends, we really don't have as much patience with one another as we used to. There is only a limited appreciation for a simple visit with one another or meaningful personal engagement. "Hey, I really want to talk to you, or I really want you to talk to me or I really want to listen to you."

My friend, David Mitchell, shared a poignant reflection with me. "There is fidelity amongst our friends, as we are always just happy to see each other. We genuinely care about each other and really have no expectations beyond that. I have always treasured this. No pretense or heirs, just friendship."

Additionally, how many of us hand write letters or cards anymore? I know many true sentiments can be shared in emails, but I recently found some letters and cards from my mother and father that were over 40 years old. I cherish those powerful treasures and words of encouragement and love. Thus, I thought it might be an intriguing book concept for not only communicating about our current or the present circumstances, but also for the benefit of future generations to know a little bit about the time and the space of which I describe.

I would like to share a quote from Mark Batterson, who wrote the book "Chasing the Lion." This book was referred to me by my close friend, Robert Mitchell Maywood, MD. Mr. Batterson certainly is a pro compared to this poor writer, but his book really drove me to think harder about many things. Here's the passage that was most influential to me. "Books are time capsules. I write because I want my great-great-grandchildren to know what I lived for and what I was willing to die for."

I remember when I was small young boy before 10 years old the many family events that I would have with the Aireys and the Gerbericks (my mom's side of the family along with the Termines). I would love (to be engaged and focus) to just observe and listen to my family members. I'd love to hear about their stories, about situations. I cherished those interactions from my grandparents, my great-grandparents, my aunts and uncles, and cousins. I really don't know if it's much appreciated in today's age. So as previously stated, I'm putting it down in word form, if not for any other purpose of perpetuity and maybe a little bit of self-gratification or maybe a sense of accomplishment.

I think I need to be fair and submit that one could argue that as a young lad I did not have much of a choice other *to be seen and not heard*, but remember no technology and social media distractions (or limitations in one sense). I'll probably share some things that nobody ever thought of, nobody ever heard about my circumstances, reflections or business advice, but I hope you enjoy the journey. And that's the most important lesson from the book; that you find your own path of steadfast awareness that you're faced with right now. I thank you for your consideration.

Steadfast Awareness: Reflections and Life's Takeaways contains many eulogies that I have written and passionately delivered and other adoring reflections concerning loved ones and friends. Their inclusion should not focus on the inevitable end of physical life, but more so on how the current people (or people of your past experiences or circumstances) and their emotional engagement affects you. I challenge the reader to really think about similar types of people and emotions in their lives and write down at least in a summary format, what are you going to do about this? Answer the question "So What?"

Please do not be offended by my Catholic, Christian, and Religious reflections. They are simply an integral part of Steadfast Awareness. I invite you to contemplate your own emotional and spiritual views after your read my reflections. Maybe you have no takeaways. That's permissible. Just complete the mental and emotional journey to determine how you think, feel, and communicate about such life events and experiences. And what you are willing to act upon; live daily.

Additionally, I have included some adult language references. These possibly reflect more of my "fight," rather than my aspiring expertise of "The King's English."

I experienced my own additional challenges while documenting this book, and I attempted to address a more personal purpose for the reader. I came up with a method to guide the reader's private thought and documentation voyage. My mind churns on these types of critical thinking examinations with the goal of crystalizing a helpful and productive approach for the reader. I do hope and pray it is worthwhile. Steadfast Awareness: Reflections and Life's Takeaways is certainly meaningful and beneficial for me to improve my being.

Your Life's Takeaways:

The chapters conclude with a Your Life's Takeaways section just for this goal. At the end of each chapter (reflections), I have included Your Life's Takeaways' questions and challenges for the reader to reflect upon and document their current conclusions. Remember, this is the book's personal challenge that I previously offered.

Additionally, I implore the reader to add, change or delete the questions in a manner of which to personalize your deliberations. I humbly submit I had to embrace a similar exercise to clearly conclude my life's takeaways, which are included in the reflections. And most importantly, write down your reflections with this book or your own journal. Please do not let the limited space on the book's pages, limit your life's takeaways or writings.

Again, thank you. Read on. Live your life.

Chapter 2: Cold Tears

"But as for that day and hour, nobody knows it, neither the angels of heaven, nor the Son, no one but the Father alone." Matthew 24:36.

In his senior years, my dad use to say gently, "No One Knows the Day or Hour."

Edmund Francis Airey, Jr.

Born: June 27, 1928. Pomona, California. Eternal Life: November 4, 2001. Fullerton, California.

Early Sunday morning at about 5 a.m. on November 4, 2001, my home phone rang next to my bed. I could tell that it was my mother's number. "Honey, the hospital called and said that something's happened your dad, "Mom said. "Can you pick me up so we can go to the hospital?" "Okay, sure mom. I'll get dressed and get right over to your home," I said with surprise.

My dad had suffered from severe diabetes and congestive heart failure since 1995. Over the past couple of years, leg and feet injuries and cuts would not heal properly. Before those challenges, dad needed two cardiovascular surgeries that entailed removing veins from the upper thigh area and re-attaching the veins to his calves to increase blood circulation. Our surgeon, William J. Foley, MD, had amazing skills. Dr. Foley's surgeries extended my dad's years and improved his quality of life.

After I hung up with my mom, I got out of bed and I told my wife, Christy, what was going on. Christy inquired, "What do you think?" I declared, "Honey, quite frankly, expect the worst." I didn't say anything else. I got up, washed my face, put in my contacts, and combed my hair, put on a white undershirt with a nice light blue button-down oxford long-sleeved shirt, and finally my jeans and tennis shoes. If I remember correctly my seven-year-old son, Garrett, (at the time) got up and stood at the bedroom doorway with his mother looking at what was going on. We all feared the worst.

I revved up my 1999 Chevy Suburban and raced over the hill to pick up my mother. My mother was dressed and ready to go. There wasn't much talking.

We arrived at Saint Jude Medical Center in Fullerton, CA and rode the elevator up to the fourth floor. There was a quite eerie feeling on the 4th floor ward. I entered into room 410. My mother sat down in a chair near the door. A blue draped curtain separated her from my father's bed. I peeked around the curtain to see my dad lying still in the bed. Now, I was aware he was dead. I grabbed my dad's hand and gently kissed it. I went back around the curtain and told my mother, "I'm sorry Mom." "I'm not ready for this, Matthew." Mom lamented. I placed my arm and hand around my mother's shoulders.

"No One Knows the Day or Hour." I could kindly hear my dad's phrase in my worried mind.

Then, a nice orderly nurse came into the room. She said, "I'm sorry." Her sensitive eyes indicated to me that she needed to clean and prepare my dad's body for removal. "OK mom let's go outside for little bit," I directed.

We eventually met the hospital chaplain priest and a few close family members to say our final goodbyes and prayers with dad. There was a somber and pensive mood, but I did add some humor by paying my last respects by re-enacting my dad's old Airey handshake. I knew in my heart I would not want to see my dad lying dead in his casket during his future mortuary viewing, so I made that my last physical tender moment with him

The handshake style was formed over years by leaning in with your right hand and right shoulder with a real strong motion, and then proceeding to give your greeter a firm handshake. My

11

dad and I always got a quick chuckle out of that handshake. So, I decided what better send off than to lean over my father and grasp his hand and shoulder. My dad's face looked so peaceful, and he had a close shave. A parting kiss on the check, just as he had shared and showed his affection toward his family and close friends. I have tried to carry on those same values with my wife, sons, family, and friends. His values included being dutiful and responsible and during his best to live up to his Catholic and American ideals.

While weeping and feeling the cold tears find their way down my face, I turned to my sister, Regina, "Look at our beautiful daddy."

My tears felt cold while running down my face. Not like the tears when you are laughing so hard you cry or when you react to a tender movie scene. These tears were empty and cold from the immediate loss of my father.

Your Life's Takeaways:

Who does this story remind you of? Write down some of the details. ____

I was 39 years old when my dad's death rocked me. My life has continued its mysterious journey after leaving hospital room 410.

How old were you when someone closed to you died? ____.

What were the surroundings, places, moods, and unique occurrences that surrounded that day? ____.

It roughly took me three years to "get over / get through" the death of my father. I still have crying emotional breakdowns when I recall all the precious memories and parental support. Have you taken the necessary time to mourn and grieve? ____.

Have you gone out of your way to seek professional and organized help? If no, maybe you should. ____.

STEADFAST AWARENESS

Take a pause now and again throughout your life (or day) to cherish someone's laugh and maybe strange but genuine demeanor. Who would that person be? ____.

I had no regrets, no anger, and no unfinished business with my dad. The only thing that I would have wished for my dad was for him to have the opportunity to prosper more and grow older. To advance within his grandsons' life and to see them playing ball and carrying on. Do you have any regrets when reflected on a lost loved one? ____.

I did have to wonder and ponder; try to understand the reason for my dad's passing at that time at the age of 73. What I do remember from that journey from hospital room 410 through those few years after my father's passing were poignant times during the weekday nights when I would read to my son, Garrett, while going to bed. I would lie down on the floor next to Garrett in his bedroom until he went to sleep. I would lay flat on my back with my arms at my side or behind my head, and I would solely stare up to the ceiling. Inevitably my mind would think about my dad and some of the different eras of his life. I also fondly recalled when dad encouraged me. These cherished emotions would overwhelm me.

What I remember about those moments was that I would start to cry maybe five or six tears from each eye. Cold tears. I wanted to feel that pain and that grief, since I figured it was part of the process to move forward. I'd let the tears run down my cheeks and past my neck, like water traversing through dry dirt, while forming its own path similar to a crevice. Those tears had power. Cold tears helped me to relax, helped me to grieve.

Can you remember such cold tears in your life? ____.

There have been a few other instances in my life I've experienced this type of concentrated grief with cold tears after the death of some friends my age or maybe just a little older; their lives ended much too soon. I'm a strong person (a strong man with some fortitude), but I attempt to force myself to experience such grieving pain, while consciously feeling cold tears running downside of my face.

Come back to this reference, if you experience such a feeling or event. List it here ____.

"No one knows the day or hour," a scripture reference as I noted previously. Some counsel to consider. Be prepared. There should be a realistic balance between hope of physical recovery and the arduous reality of one physical and emotional aliments. This is difficult to clarify, but I am referencing the connection between the body and mind and that such aliments both need to heal.

You never really know when a family member or friend is truly in danger, in harm's way, or close to their demise. You may not be briefed in advance if one of your managers, coworkers or team members suffers a significant loss within their own immediate family or with their own physical or emotional state. Take a pause. Stop and think about what is and not happening. Why did this happen? Figure out the way to best support the person, group, or yourself who experienced a loss of a family member, friend or of an emotional aliment.

List a circumstance that comes to mind here ____.
What did you do? ____.
What were you thinking / experiencing? ____.

Additional advice / reflection: Seek professional help. A stigmatism exists about seeking professional help, psychological help, or medical help for the grieving process (or a mental ailment). But avoidance of such support can bear long term and unproductive consequences, such as pervasive anxiety and harmful physical impacts to weight, blood pressure, and sleep. I certainly advocate religious grieving counselors in that process. It was helpful to me.

STEADFAST AWARENESS

But be aware and sensitive to your own needs and style. I think the most detrimental path folks can walk is not to ponder and think about what actually happened or is happening. According to Socrates: "The unexamined life is not worth living." You need to think about these painful times, but do not to be paralyzed; be somewhat analytical. Analysis with the goal of forming a plan (maybe baby steps) of moving forward through grief by recalling great memories, great advice, and great values of your loved one.

How did they live their life? List your thoughts here ____.

List your plan to move forward ____.

What are the three key words that summarize your plan? ____.

Part of your Steadfast Awareness and Your Life's Takeaways may or may not include cold tears. My cold tears represented another level of physical awareness of my grieving process. Maybe similar to experiencing the pain from an injury or enduring the pain of regaining one's physical strength. Or the stamina of people pushing through medical treatments.

List your reflections regarding your process here? ____.

Reflecting back on viewing my father on his death bed. I observed that he did not have one of his earthly possessions on his person, not even his Timex watch. Please remember your reflections / your process is on its own time frame, your timeframe alone.

List timeframe (for example, days, weeks, months, years) of Your Life's Takeaways and goals. ____.

Chapter 3: "We Only Make It Complex."

Edmund Francis Airey, Jr. was born at Pomona Hospital, California on June 27, 1928. He was raised on the Airey Ranch in Walnut and attended St. Joseph's Parochial School in Pomona. His high school days were spent at Loyola High School in Los Angeles from which he graduated in 1946. That fall he entered the Catholic Junior Seminary and continued onto St. John's Seminary in Camarillo, California, receiving his Bachelor of Arts degree in Philosophy in 1950. Ed continued his theology studies at St. John's Seminary, but he decided to leave the seminary in 1953.

Ed was then drafted into the US Army and served from 1954 to 1956. He enrolled at Loyola University in Los Angeles, and he completed his Master of Education and Teaching Credential in 1958. Ed taught for one year at La Puente High School before beginning his 33-year teaching and counseling career at Los Altos High School in Hacienda Heights, California. He taught English, Latin, Remedial Reading, and Adult School and was an attendance counselor before retiring in 1992.

While growing up on the Airey Ranch in Walnut, California Ed raised rabbits and chickens. He loved animals and farming and even in later years worked summers and weekends on the family ranch. He was witty and friendly and cared about all people and their spirituality. Ed volunteered countless hours to various schools and charities, such as Bishop Amat High School Boosters, Manresa Retreats, Catholic Charities, and Pomona Valley Farmers' Market.

Ed is survived by his wife, Marguerite, whom he married on June 24, 1961, at St. Luke in Temple City, California. His son, Matthew, daughter-in-law, Christy, and daughter, Regina, also survive him. Ed has three grandsons, Garrett, Shane, and Connor. He was the second oldest of nine children. His surviving brothers and sisters include (as of November 12, 2001) Marie Therese, Jean, Mary Lou, Joe, Patty, and Adrienne. His sister, Sister Margaret of the Sisters of the Holy Names, and his brother, Thomas Patrick, predeceased Ed. Ed passed away on November 4, 2001.

Chapter Introduction: The first church eulogy I delivered was for my grandfather, Edmund Francis Airey, Sr., in July 1992. I still cannot find my original text that I wrote, but I pray to Saint Anthony that one day I will find it. That probability is most likely small.

I made certain I then started to physically save a copy and computer file save such memorable writings.

November 12, 2001 – Veteran's' Day. Eulogy of Edmund Francis Airey, Jr. by Matthew Edmund Airey.
St. Denis Catholic Church, Diamond Bar, California.

My dad once made a duck egg omelet for his brother, Jean, and he never told him. His brother said it looked kind of greasy.

My dad had a funny way of sharing his faith with some of his army buddies when a funny prank scared them to call for the Lord's help. One late night some of the fellas stumbled into the dark barracks after a night on the town. My dad had one of those novelty cans that when you tipped it over, it sounded exactly like a cow mooing. When my dad tipped it over, the response from the fellas was, "Jesus Christ. Oh, My God, there's a cow in the barracks."

My Papa Jim, my maternal grandfather, James Henry Gerberick, had one of those rubber chickens that my dad borrowed. Dad once put the rubber chicken under my pillow. He also placed the rubber chicken in between some coats in the front closet. I am sure that rubber chicken may cross your path some time as well.

Just one more funny story. My friend, Jim Duffy, was over visiting one night, and my dad commented: "Jimmy, you're getting pretty big."

"Why, yes, I am, Mr. Airey." How much do you think I weigh?"

"265," my dad quickly replied.

"That's right. How did you know that?

My dad replied, "I used to judge cattle for a living."

Names

People are known by many names. And my dad was no exception. I hope these names help all of us to remember a certain moment or flash back, that we can carry forward.

Monk. This was due to his sister, Marie Therese, not being able to pronounce Edmund correctly as a young girl. This later lead to Uncle Monk and Uncle Monka.

Other names included: Edmundo Segundo, Junior, Eddie, Chet, Tex, Mr. Airey the Teacher and Counselor, Manresa Retreat Captain. (Note: Manresa was a Retreat Center run by the Jesuit Priests in Azusa, California, and my dad would recruit men to attend a three-day spiritual retreat away from their daily demands.)

A Brother of the Sack. This referred to the unique religious order of pulling the covers over one's head in bed. (Please note: This is a fictitious humorous reference only; not a religious order.)

Brute force. His seminary buddies referred to his farm boy strength.

He was a 2-time winner of catching the Greased Pig at local festivals. The secret technique was to grab the pig's hind legs.

Son, Brother, Friend, Husband, Beautiful Daddy, Papa.

Ask What, Not Why

At a sorrowful time like this, we naturally ask the question why.

The real question to ask is what.

I learned this lesson, in of all places, Las Vegas. While visiting Vegas with some friends, I dragged myself out of bed on Sunday morning, and I ran up the Strip to Mass. When I got to the church, it was packed. I quickly remembered the story from Uncle Joe Airey's friend's advice, "Joe, there's some extra seats in the choir." And sure enough, there were. The priest gave a moving homily about the way to look a death. The priest preached when encountering death, ask what, not why.

The Lord had a challenging way to prepare me for this day and the days ahead. You see, my four-year-old son, Connor, did not sleep through the night until he turned three. Since it was tough to wake up several times a night, I began to pray while fulfilling my fatherly duties. I would say a Hail Mary for my Dad, a Hail Mary for all the priests, sisters, and religious, and a Hail Mary that my son would go back to sleep. ... No, it was really a prayer for all of my family.

I always found myself reverting back to some perspective or memory of my dad. Here are some of my thoughts that will hopefully help us to continue to celebrate his life and ours, and to live by his example.

My thoughts reflect upon my dad being special, being thankful, providing fond memories with powerful messages, giving encouragement, Ed by the numbers, Prayer and Action, and Life's Simplicity.

Special

Twenty years ago, when I was 19, I was over at Jimmy Duffy's house, and Jim's Dad, Mr. Duffy, asked me how my dad was doing. My dad referred to Mr. Duffy as Big Jim, since he was the older Duffy and due to his tough sprinkler fitter stature. Instead of answering Mr. Duffy's question, I started complaining about my dad. Mr. Duffy replied softly, but firmly, "Don't say that about your father. He's a very special man."

There are moments in one's life that provide crystal precise meaning. That was one of those moments for me. My dad was a special man because he focused on Faith and Family.

Thank Yous

My dad believed in thanking those around him, because he loved them. So, in that spirit, I want to express heartfelt gratitude to some of those, who were around in my father's life.

My dad's biography mentioned that he raised rabbits and chickens. I still don't know why, but his endearment for my mother was the nickname, "chicken." **May dad loved my mother, and I know he was so very grateful for her being so steadfast during their life together and his health challenges.**

It was my Mom, quiet Marguerite, who told the doctors about hyper-barrack chamber treatments. My mom was the interconvert, and my dad the extrovert. But Marguerite would always speak up for the right cause and moment, such as using innovating medical treatments. The Mayo Clinic noted "Hyperbaric oxygen therapy involves breathing pure oxygen in a tube ... the therapy treats serious infections, bubbles of air in your blood vessels, and wounds that won't heal as a result of diabetes." This treatment turned out to be the start of just one of many miracles. Thank you, Mom.

STEADFAST AWARENESS

My dad would always say, "Your sister, Gina is so smart." I would say, "Yeah, I know Dad." But the most poignant conversation I ever had with dad about my sister was during the night we found out Gina had cancer in 1981. I was just about to drift off to sleep, and my dad came into my bedroom and sat at the edge of my bed. I could tell he was anxious and wanted to talk, since we were worried about his daughter. I started to focus because I felt my dad's distress.

He asked, "Why do you think Gina has cancer? Is it the water we drink or the food we eat?" I could not answer my father's intense questions. I just consoled him and said, "Jeez dad, I don't know dad. I just think if we hope and pray, Gina will be alright." And she was and is. Thank you, Gina.

Dad loved his daughter-in-law, Christy, he marveled at her ability to be a schoolteacher, a wife, and a loving mother. He used to say, "Well, ya know, Christy's pretty efficient." Thank you, Christy. Dad marveled a Christy capable manner to get ready to teach her classes, get the boys ready for school, and maintain organized home.

He loved his parents, who gave him an appreciation of family, church, and education. I remember dad telling me that his father, Papa, cut a deal with the Jesuits, because he could not afford the full tuition at Loyola High School. He thought that Papa did not finish paying off his tuition for Loyola High School until years after he graduated. Thank you, Mama and Papa. (Side note: I fondly remember this memory 12 years later when I found myself "cutting a deal" for my sons' tuition.)

My dad loved and prayed for all of his brothers, sisters, nieces, nephews, godchildren, confirmation candidates, doctors, health care providers, and friends. Thank you all for your prayers, generosity, and support.

My dad would also tell me, "Now, tell the boys to thank their teachers."

My dad just recently told me a story about being an eighth grader at St. Joseph's in Pomona. The story began, "Since I was one of the smartest ones in the class .... The sisters would let him walk down the street to the convent and bring back their lunch. My dad appreciated a memory of that simple school experience. Thank you to all of my dad's teachers, religious ministry, and his fellow teachers.

Special thanks to Monsignor Jim Loughnane, Father Mike, Father Gene, and Father Rod. (Note: Monsignor Jim was the pastor of St. Denis Church and was very welcoming to my parents with his Irish charm and wisdom. Father Michael Engh, SJ was my father's oldest nephew. Father Gene and Father Rod were St. John's Seminary College {Camarillo, CA} classmates of my father. My dad kept in touch with many of his college friends, who had become priests.)

My dad left the seminary because he didn't sense that the seminary taught enough compassion and personal interaction with the community. But these men are truly humble servants of our Lord. They focus on others, not themselves. Their supportive behaviors are consistent and caring. Thank you.

One of my dad's closest seminary classmates was Bishop Juan Arzube. "Juanito" could not be at this funeral, but I remember the profound blessing Bishop Juan gave my dad and me outside of the church prior to my marriage ceremony. I felt time stopped. I felt the Lord's power at that time. Thank you, Bishop Juan.

You see that experience wouldn't have happened without my dad's intervention. As I told him, so many times before, and I am telling him today - Thank you, dad. I love you.

You were powerful while you were here on earth. I am sure you will be even more powerful in heaven.

Fond Memories with Powerful Life Messages

Now, let me share some fond memories with powerful life messages.

My dad would always drop us off at St. Martha's School with an affectionate kiss. One day I asked him to cool it, because the guys were teasing me about it. Not soon after that, out of the blue, my friend, Jimmy, asked me why I didn't kiss my dad anymore. "Who's going to make fun of us? We're the biggest guys on campus." Jimmy advised. I quickly reversed my request of dad and welcomed his affection. And I never missed a chance to kiss my dad since.

My dad was sensitive and emotional as well. The earliest and most powerful example of this was the day my Nana Josephine (my mother's mother, my grandmother) died on June 9, 1972. My dad led Gina and I upstairs to my mom and dad's bedroom, and he sat at the edge of the bed. He told us that Papa Jim (my mother's father, my grandfather) had called him at school and that "Your Nana died." Before he could get to the end of the sentence, he busted into tears. These tears were the tears of emotion and love and sorrow for his wife losing her mother at the young age of 62. I remember the powerful impact of my dad's behavior on me that day. And unfortunately, I relived that emotion years later, when I heard my friend, Matt Zuro, eulogized his "superb mother."

I remember the day my Aunt Peggy (Sister Margaret Airey) died in 1974. My mom, Gina, and I greeted my dad at the door with a hug as he arrived back from work, and we told him the bad news. He smiled and said, "Her suffering is now over."

This reminds me of a time when he was driving me in the car east on the 60 freeway, and we were just having a general conversation. As we got off on Nogales, he said, "What makes life worth living is heaven." Boom, there was another of those powerful messages. Dad was saying the ultimate prize is the afterlife versus the challenges on earth.

More Memories from My Youth

When I was about 8, my dad would let me fall asleep in his bed. Dad would kid me, "Jeez, Matthew, you're getting pretty big to be in here." Being next to him gave me a true sense of belonging.

I remember kneeling by my mom and dad's bed and praying the rosary on Good Friday.

My parents taught me about my patron, Saint Matthew, and his feast day on September 21. People who have the same name as a saint may consider the saint their patron. Catholic (and European) tradition holds that a patron saint spiritually intercedes for a person's protection and guidance. Saint Matthew is the Patron Saint of: Accountants, Actors, Bankers, Bookkeepers, and

Tax collectors. Interesting, sounds similar to the author's interests (me).

One Saturday afternoon while driving down Holt Boulevard in Pomona, we stopped at St. Joseph's Church to make a visit and to kiss a small replica of our Lord's crucifix. Powerful messages.

At my Uncle Joe's wedding in 1969, my dad was the one who finally got Uncle Andre's Model T Ford "crank started" to allow the bride and the groom to flee to the reception party. Andre was my grandfather Airey's grammar school chum, who had a sister who would become his bride, my grandmother. Andre had a talent for restoring and maintaining old vintage cars. The Model T's engine was turned on (or turned over) by using a crank. You would use your left hand to crank the lever (if the engine backfires and the lever swings counterclockwise, the left arm is less likely to be broken). So, my dad gave it a vigorous half-crank, and the engine started. I remember thinking ... "Hey, that's my dad."

I remember he would throw the football to me in our back yard. I would slant across the middle of the yard to catch his pass. I can just see the white and blue Los Angeles Rams vinyl football coming right over my right shoulder into my hands. Oh, how I loved that time with him.

I once caught him off guard when I paid him a surprise visit at his summer school class. He looked at me and smiled. Stopped his lesson and asked the class to just hold on a second. Dad stepped outside the classroom door and said, "Hey, Matt." "Hey dad, I was over at Hank's house and thought I would stop by and say hi," I replied. Again, he appreciated the short visit and said, "Thanks. See you at home."

My dad had "big banana fingers" from working with his hands at the Airey Ranch since his youth. The Airey Ranch in Walnut, California is my Father's family homestead, citrus grove, farm fields, and livestock pastures since 1927. Dad had a unique handshake to go with his thick fingers. When Dad would shake your hand, he would swing out his elbow and move his shoulder toward you. Even Father Don Duplessis, OSM our Servite Friar Priest friend would get a big laugh from Dad's handshake.

All fond memories with powerful messages. Another time when I was 23, I was complaining about some trivial life challenge I was encountering, and he said, "God gave you big shoulders to help you handle your problems." This advice helped me carry on then, and today. I listened to a friend tell me about his turmoil at work. Well, I'll give you the same advice my dad gave me years ago. "God gave you big shoulders to help you handle your problems." My friend later communicated that the advice rang true for him as well as for me.

Encouragement During My Bishop Amat High School Years

Here are some examples of encouragement via my dad.

Before I started Bishop Amat, my dad encouraged me to introduce myself to the school chaplain, Father John Patrick Cremins. My dad said that he knew Fr. Cremins from teaching music in the seminary. I remember walking down the freshmen hallway, and I saw Father walking towards me. I extended my hand and said, "I am Matt Airey. My dad told me I should meet you." Father smiled, shook my hand, and put his other hand on my shoulder and said, "I know you, and I know your family. I used to give your Aunt Peggy communion."

Besides my parents and sister, Fr. Cremins was the single most influential person on my life. Father would say, "God's generosity cannot be outdone." My dad's goodness was part of God's generosity.

Fr. Cremins also taught me how to be a man who lives what we are called to do. To understand one's call in life, you need to be aware of your present circumstances, strengths, weaknesses, and opportunity. It helps to be silent in personal prayer as one becomes cognizant of the present moment and opportunities to better oneself and address challenges. Father noted a man (or women) faces his challenges head on with a plan of action. It may take some time, maybe years, and some hard work, but it can support your destined vocations. Lastly, in 1994 Bishop Ward eulogized Fr. Cremins with this final quote, "Certainly, this priest was Jesus' face in person on earth."

You see that experience wouldn't have happened without my dad's encouragement and life's connections.

During my sophomore year, I remember after running the football for a big gain, I could single out my dad's cheer from the stands, as I got up from the tackled pile ... "Good boy."

Finally, my dad wrote many recommendations for kids to be accepted into Amat. In fact, while he was in post-op for a recent surgery on his leg, he called me in the hospital waiting room. "Dad, how are you?" I asked. "Oh, I am fine. Hey, Matt, talk to this nurse. She's thinking of sending her son to Amat." That was just one of thousands of examples of his selflessness and his promotion of Amat.

Ed, By the Numbers

I call this section, Ed by the numbers.

He had many godchildren.

He invested time in sponsoring confirmation candidates.

He confidently and confidentially attracted hundreds of men to attend Manresa retreats.

He sold hundreds of ads for high school programs, created programs, and then enthusiastically sold them.

He volunteered thousands of hours to various schools and charities.

He introduced himself to hundreds of people for the first time with a warm smile.

He educated thousands of students.

He gave away thousands of grapefruits from the Airey Ranch grove, since the family did not actively harvest the remaining small orchid. So, my dad would walk through the grove and pick a couple of bags of grapefruit and travel around to family friends to distribute them.

Dad gave away thousands of golf balls he gathered from Airey Ranch orchard due to inaccurate golfers along the Fairway Avenue golf course. He walked a million miles in the orchard and on the Airey Ranch.

He traveled thousands of times to Pomona, Los Angeles, San Gabriel, Hacienda Heights, La Puente, and Walnut.

Pray and Action

You know that my dad was a man of action, but he believed prayer initialized action.

A Prayer from Saint Augustine summarized it for him, "Pray as though everything depended on God. Work as though everything depended on you."

During his freshmen year at Loyola High School in 1942, my dad often felt lonely because he was 27 miles away from his childhood surroundings and family, while staying with his maternal grandparents in Culver City, California. To ease his strife, he began to pray to Father Junípero Serra, the founder of the California Missions. His prayers were answered when his younger brother, Jean, was able to skip the eighth grade and accompany my dad during his next three years of high school starting in 1943.

My dad would also tell me, "Now, tell the boys to do something nice for someone each day." That is why he took such an interest in people, and their lives were touched because of him.

I remember my dad sharing a story about a meaningful experience he had while counseling a student with a poor attendance record. During my dad's discussion with the student, he asked, "Are your parents ever around?" The painful look on the student's face answered my dad's question. My dad felt so sorry for the student, and he said the kid almost started crying. My dad had a hard time believing someone's lack of involvement, especially regarding their precious children.

My dad never complained about his health challenges and length of stay in the hospital. I would tell him that he was so brave. Now, we have to do the same and pray, but also act and do. We need to listen, console, reconcile, and increase our compassion for others. In essence, bear witness to our Lord's word and do his work, now, so we may see clearly our Lords' face in heaven.

Finally, there are complexities in life, but life is not complex. We only make it complex.

Here are my final 3 simple examples of my dad's legacy and his appreciation for life's joys.

My dad would refer to his seven-year-old grandson's athletic talent as "God given." He relished the chance to retell others that Garrett scored three goals in one soccer game. My dad would ask, "How many goals do you think Garrett scored?" "Three of the four goals." He would quickly reply.

Before my dad's last leg vein surgery, we were in his room giving him some encouragement. Since we just kept waiting and waiting, Aunt Mary and Uncle Jean asked me to give them an update on our boys. My update gave my dad and all of us a hearty laugh and the encouragement my dad needed.

I told them our son, Shane, was somewhat of a dramatic evangelist even at only 5 years old. I told them that recently during our family "quiet time" before going to bed, Shane spontaneously decided to stand up on the family room coffee table and intensely preach about the Lord's resurrection. Shane powerfully raised his hands to heaven and proclaimed, "The Lord had risen from the dead." Shane continued as he actively pointed at our family congregation, "The Lord is alive, and He is alive in you, and in you, and in you."

Lastly, on All Saints Day, Connor came home from pre-school signing a song that immediately made me think of my dad.

My dad loved Connor's smile, and Connor was smiling so proudly when he sang his song to his Papa on the telephone that night.

I'm gonna sing, sing, sing
I'm gonna shout, shout, shout
Praise the Lord.
When the gates are open wide, I'm gonna sit by Jesus' side.

I'm gonna sing, sing, sing

I'm gonna shout, shout, shout

Praise the Lord.

When the gates are open wide, I'm gonna sit by Jesus' side.

Your Life's Takeaways:

Reflect on a loved one's simple characteristics and generosity.

List them here ____.

List how many lives that one person has impacted ____.

What parts of your life (things) have you made too complex? List them here ____.

Complex to Simple: What can you do to simplify your life, your daily routine, and your relationship to others? ____.

It really does not take much to live a fulfilling life. List the non-complex actions you will take to simplify your life and your perspectives. ____.

Chapter 4: "A Tree, A Team, and A Testimony"

Homily for the Funeral of Edmund Francis Airey, Jr.

St. Denis Church, Diamond Bar, California

12 November 2001

Written and Delivered by Michael Engh, SJ. Reprinted with permission from the author.

Today we gather to bid farewell to Ed Airey – husband, father, grandfather, brother, uncle, and friend. To Marguerite, Gina, Matthew and Christy, and to your children - to each of you we extend our support, our love, and our sympathy for your loss. Our presence today is a tribute to this man whom you cherished, and a heartfelt expression of our care and regard for each of you. Reflecting on the readings you selected, three thoughts came to mind, three points that touch on God's message for us today: A Tree, A Team, and A Testimony.

To begin. A Tree.

On the day that Ed died, I was out walking at dawn, along the banks of the Cooper River, outside of Philadelphia. The sunlight played across all the trees, particularly on one maple, with brilliant red and yellow leaves. A strong cold breeze hit the tree, and soon hundreds of leaves cart-wheeled and somersaulted through the air and rained like confetti at a New Year's Eve party. The river carried the leaves away, as autumn claimed the year's growth, and left the tree stark and barren.

As I later learned, on that same morning, at that same time, three thousand miles away, Ed Airey died as the new day dawned. Sunlight of a different kind played brilliantly on him, the light of the Son of God who is not limited by the annual change of seasons. The wind that blew that day was no autumn blast, but the breath of God's Holy Spirit that carried Ed from our midst. No icy river swallowed Ed in death, because the waters into which he had plunged were Baptism's living waters that flow from the side of Christ.

The image of the tree lingered as I recalled this man who was raised in a home set amongst a citrus grove and who tended that orchard for so many years. Ed knew those trees well, where he disked weeds and irrigated the terraces. Ed, however, was far more familiar with the Tree of Life, the Cross of Jesus, where he cultivated his belief in Jesus Christ, through prayer, Communion, and retreats. He tended that Tree all his life. By sharing his faith with his children and grandchildren, that Tree flourished anew for two more generations in this branch of the Airey family.

Like pruning for new growth, Ed's long months in the hospital gave him ample time to reflect on life, struggle with his pain, and deepen his faith. He could see what could be cut, what mattered most in life. Visiting him a month ago, I caught a brief glimpse of what his priorities were. First, he called Marguerite to tell her of the visit. Then, he phoned Matt, and we talked. Next, he spoke with affection about Christy, and he showed me the artwork that Garrett, Shane, and Connor created for his hospital room. He wanted then to tell me all about Gina. He shared a prayer from Mother Teresa, and when it came to time to say farewell, he asked for a blessing. In the light of the Tree of Life, Ed had determined his priorities and he knew what mattered most.

A Team.

In his prayer and in a lifetime of living the Faith, Ed had discovered what Jesus meant in our Gospel today, "My yoke is easy, and my burden is light." The yoke of faith fit him comfortably. It did not pinch or chaff, scrape or cut. But a yoke links two in a team for work.

One writer who explained this image very well is the late Cardinal Joseph Bernardin, Archbishop of Chicago. Many of you are familiar with his profound book, The Gift of Peace that he wrote while he faced his own illness, pancreatic cancer. Cardinal Bernardin counted this Gospel passage as one of his favorites. In his chapter titled, "Befriending Death," he explains why this Gospel passage meant so much to him:

> "Usually a yoke joined a pair of oxen and made them a team. It is as though Jesus tells us, 'Walk alongside me; learn to carry the burdens by observing how I do it. If you let me help you, the heavy labor will seem lighter.' ...But notice that Jesus did not promise to take away our burdens. He promised to help us carry them. And if we let go of ourselves – and our own resources – and allow the Lord to help us, we will be able to see death not as an enemy or a threat but as a friend." (p. 126)

Being tied to the Lord eased Ed's burdens and strengthened him for every difficulty. He walked alongside of Jesus and kept in step, as best he could. His struggle with diabetes, his months of hospitalization, and his slow healing taxed him in body and soul. And yet he persevered. He clung to his faith. What Isaiah wrote in our first reading, Ed prayed: "This is our God, we trusted in him." Trusting in God, he found his burden bearable because shared the pain with the Lord. He was teamed with Jesus.

A Testimony.

Which brings up the third thought. This witness, this model of persevering faith is Ed's legacy to his family and his lasting gift to us. Ed's example of faith throughout his life is his testimony. It reminds us that God hears our pain, shares our joys, and eases our burdens. It also reminds us that God, after all, is not deaf. Ed believed, and found his prayers answered through God's abiding presence. We who gather here this morning pray for Ed's rest in the Lord, for the consolation of his family, and for our own discovery of God's faithful presence. We pray that we too can see what Ed came to know in his heart. We ask that we, also, might hear God's footsteps alongside our own.

Let me conclude. If Ed's death brings us closer to knowing God's presence and care, then we will find blessings even in this time of sorrow. If we can see how God teams up with us, we are closer to letting God help with our daily burdens. If we learn from Ed's testament of faith, then the Tree of Life will sink deeper roots in our own hearts. We celebrate the new life that Ed enjoys, and we pray for the consolation of Marguerite, Gina, Matt and Christy. God bless you in your grief and thank you for the love that supported Ed and enabled him to persevere in his example for us of a valiant, steadfast faith.

Your Life's Takeaways:

Father Michael used his experience of the tree to illustrate Ed's (my dad's) life.

What example in nature reminds you of someone living or passed on? ____.

Who is on your team? ____.

Does your faith or belief system influence your team, such as the reflection referenced in the above text? ____.

Who are the people on your team, who support your daily adventures? ____.

What is your current testimony? ____.

Is your testimony what you currently want it to be? ____.

What do you need to change in your life now to get back on track? ____.

And what is actually positively and productively working in your current testimony? ____.

What do you hope your testimony will be when you are faced with life's severe struggles? ____.

Share a testimony of a close family member, friend, or acquaintance that you admire and value? ____.

How does that apply to your current life? ____.

Chapter 5: "Quiet Heart"

Introduction: I am not a poet or songwriter. Maybe not even a writer ... ha ha, but I find that I am sometimes inspired to write down my reflections, thoughts, and emotions within a poetic style. Poems provide a concise format to simply record the significant phrases and themes that should have meaning or references to the subject and author. I truly admire the expressions and imagines that songwriters weave into their lyrics. Some songwriters start with a simple "musical riff" and catchphrase (maybe the chorus that repeats), and then build the lyrics around a concept or storyline.

I wrote this poem for my mom on her 70th birthday at a time when she and I were still grieving over my dad's death just 18 months prior, and while she was still formulating her daily schedule. What do I do now? What should I do now? I recall I was reflecting on my mom and her past life, life with my dad, life with her two children, her characteristics, and emotions for the future. My mind just wondered around and eventually focused on a few items, and then I summarize them on paper.

My mom was an introvert but a comprehensive thinker that I referred to as a "Quiet Heart."

For Marguerite June (Gerberick) Airey on Her 70th Birthday – June 4, 2003

Quiet Heart

Quiet Heart, from my very first day,
Quiet Heart, with me today,
Quiet Heart, to cherish ever more.

Steadfast Awareness

Long ago a young girl would be,
Loved by two, true to thee.

She was dark haired and eyed,
And learned well, quiet, and shy.
She sang songs fun, sang them loud,
Her family and all were proud.

Quiet Heart, from my very first day,
Quiet Heart, with me today,
Quiet Heart, to cherish ever more.

Took steps toward her dreams,
Some of which were seldom seen.

Worked to enable her school reading,
And kept at it, kept leading.

Leading down a long road, a drive away,
To complete one goal, leading toward today.

Quiet Heart, from my very first day,
Quiet Heart, with me today,
Quiet Heart, to cherish ever more.

Years pasted and her love grew,
To share the quiet heart, only she knew.

This fine heart knew the joy, pain, the kindness,
Of good family, children; the tenderness.

Quiet Heart, from my very first day,
Quiet Heart, with me today,
Quiet Heart, to cherish ever more.

This Quiet Heart needs to give and love long,
so
Younger Hearts have the chance to learn life's quiet song.

Your Life's Takeaways:

Have you ever written a poem or a story after reflecting on your current life or the fine qualities of a loved one or friend? ____.

When was that? ____.
Where is that poem now? ____.
Can you recreate it? Or summarize your feelings? ____.

If you had the chance to write a poem about someone regarding your current feelings, what would you say? Can you write down those words to express those emotions now? ____.

What are phrases and themes that come to mind (i.e. pop into your head)? Can you capture those words and write them down? ____.

What are the most accurate words to express your thoughts? ____.

Chapter 6: "Gratitude. Formation. Legacy."

In Loving Memory of Marguerite June Airey. June 4, 1933 – January 6, 2020

European and Californian Roots.

Marguerite June Gerberick was born on June 4, 1933, in Fresno, CA. Her father, James Henry Gerberick (AKA Jim, Dad, Uncle Jimmy) was a truck driver (Teamster) who was born in 1908 in Washington State, the grandson of German immigrants who had settled in Pennsylvania before heading West. Her mother, Josephine Termine (AKA Josie, Mother, Aunt Jo) was born in Independence, Louisiana, in 1911, the second of six children of immigrants from Sicily, south of Palermo. Nana Sarah (Candiotta) immigrated to the US in 1896 from a town now known as Piana degli Albanesi; Papa Sam (Salvatore) immigrated in 1906 from Palazzo Adriano. Josephine and her family moved to Los Angeles in the 1920's for better opportunities and weather. Josephine was employed as an "egg candler (Before factory automation, a worker would hold each egg up to the light and determine that a chick was not beginning to form.)" when she met a handsome and playful delivery driver. Jim and Josie were married in 1930 and moved to Fresno for Jim's new truck driving job.

What's in a Name?

Marguerite's namesake was her father's younger sister, Marguerite Gerberick, who had tragically passed away in a car accident. Baby Marguerite grew to be very artistic and creative just like her aunt had been. Drawings, cartoons, poetry, radio plays, short stories, and even a historical novel would all be in little Marguerite's future. When they were stumped for a middle name, Nana Sarah suggested June – the birth month. Two years after Marguerite's birth, her only sibling arrived: George Samuel Gerberick was named after his paternal grandfathers.

From School Girl to School Teacher.

During WWII (1940s), Marguerite and her family moved to the San Gabriel Valley where she spent the rest of her years except for later college. They lived in Alhambra (with Jim Gerberick's parents), followed by San Gabriel, then Rosemead. Marguerite worshiped at All Souls Catholic Church in Alhambra and was confirmed there. Her sponsor was Lee Alfano, who became her fellow catechism teacher and lifelong friend. Education was very important to her and her parents, especially since they had not had the opportunity to complete high school. She was a top student, graduating from Alhambra High School in 1951. Marguerite then attended Pasadena City College and worked as a tutor and park recreation supervisor. With the support of local relatives, she moved south to attend San Diego State University, where she received her bachelor's degree and teaching credential in 1956.

Marguerite taught at Temple City High School until 1961; her favorite era to explore with students was US colonial history. She saved her money and took adventurous summer trips for teachers: Crossing the Atlantic by ship and touring Western Europe by car for two months, and later exploring Hawaii before it became a state. The seeds were planted for the love of travel that she would instill in her kids and the cruises of her retirement.

She and Lee enjoyed Catholic Young Alumni dances and events, which is where she met Edmund Francis Airey, Jr. (from the Airey Ranch, Walnut, CA) in 1960. Ed was a fellow high school teacher (at La Puente and Los Altos High Schools), and the second of nine children from a devout Catholic family of English, Irish and French descent.

Mom and Nana.

Ed and Marguerite were married at Saint Luke's Catholic Church in Temple City, CA, on a hot summer day (June 24, 1961). The couple lived in a small rented house on Walnut Grove Avenue in San Gabriel. Both of their children (Matthew Edmund and Regina Marie) were born at Saint Luke's Hospital in Pasadena. In October 1967, the Aireys moved their young family into a new home in Walnut that would be Marguerite's nest and canvas for over 52 years. She immersed in the daily practices of making a home and nurturing a family, sending everyone out the door looking sharp and feeling confident they were ready for school.

Marguerite had wide interests including reading, music, television, movies, musical theater, current local and world events, travel, gardening, and home decorating. She painted her home with flora: flowers, succulents, plants, and trees abounded inside and outside. Her exceptional "green thumb" was part innate artistic sensibilities and part spiritual connection to God's creation.

Marguerite was so happy to see her son marry Christy Abbott in 1992 and overjoyed to be "Nana" to three grandsons (Garrett Matthew, Shane Abbott, Connor James) - nurturing, guiding, and praying for them always. She proudly attended all her grandsons' sporting, school, and graduation events.

Resilience and New Adventures.

While her 40 years of marriage shaped her adult life, the last 18 have been quite full. She'd reawakened her love of cruising when she and Ed took their first voyage through the Panama Canal: They were captivated. After his passing in 2001, Marguerite fulfilled Ed's desire to cruise with Gina to Alaska. With her willing cruise buddy, she checked off her bucket list: South Pacific islands from Tahiti to Australia, and autumn colors from Montreal to New York.

Despite her health challenges over the more recent years, she remained "Sweet Marguerite" (one of her many enduring nicknames), relishing the simple pleasures of reading and snuggling with her cats, and enjoying most when she could be with her extended family.

Love and Prayers.

We end this just as she closed each card and letter… We love you Mom/Nana/Auntie. We know your "Love and Prayers" are with us still and forever.

A Tribute from Her Grandsons

Today and always we remember our Nana, Marguerite Airey.

We recall the countless times she would pick us up from St. Juliana School in her Ford Taurus after school, and we would head to the nearest El Pollo Loco and other restaurants. Then, we would watch the local news at her home and eat ice cream Bon Bons for dessert.

We reflect on all the holidays we spent with Nana – coin-filled Easter egg hunts and lots of Christmas presents – plus countless sessions of arts and crafts and baking. We cherish our games of Bocce Ball (Italian lawn bowling) in her yard. And during the times when we would get too rough, Nana would cut off a stem of her Aloe Vera plant to soothe our scratches.

Even as we got older, Nana would love to hear about all our high school and college subjects and our countless sporting events and accomplishments. Her encouragement and interest in our lives and activities is something we will reflect on often.

We will forever be grounded by the foundation of education, informative garden tours, social and political awareness, the Catholic Faith, kindness, and love she instilled in us.

We love our Nana and know she is and will always be looking over us.

– Garrett (25), Shane (23), Connor (22)

January 18, 2020. Eulogy of Marguerite June Airey by Matthew Edmund Airey.
Saint Elizabeth Ann Setan Catholic Church, Rowland Heights, California.

Thank you all for being here. My mother would say thank you. I love you all. And I know Marguerite loves you too. Mom, I love you.

I know that some of you here are actively supporting loved ones, who suffer from the pains of growing older. Such was the case in the nearly last four years with my mom and her dementia. And when you are dealing with this circumstance, I found that a lot of love and some humor can go a long way.

My mother was an extremely intelligent person. But one time when I was visiting her, she expressed her intense frustration directly to me. "Matthew, I don't know anything about my mail, my bills, or anything." I took pause, and I was sad. But I smiled and said, "Ma, you're retired, and you don't have to worry about anything. And besides, you got the best secretary and treasurer, and you don't pay him anything." My Mom grinned, "I am pretty smart, aren't I."

Yes, she was smart with her "zingers," and she was a Bright History Teacher. Mom would read the Los Angeles Times daily and watch the daily nightly world news. Our daily telephone calls would cover a range and realm of topics. And mom would conclude, "Well, now that we solved the world's problems. Night. Night."

Mom would also read Victorian romance novels with titles like The Duchess of Desire and The Passionate Duke. I would open one of her books up to any page and start dramatically reading it out loud. "Stop it, that's my book." Good Humor.

This church has a meaningful family history. And my mom loved history. My mom and dad walked down the aisle here with me on my wedding day. My sister, sister in laws, brother in law, and friends here today were in the wedding party. Father Mike married us. My wife, Christy, and I attended RCIA (Rite of Christian Initiation of Adults) classes here. Gina eulogized Mama Airey here. And I eulogized my grandfather here, who helped to build this church. (Note: My grandfather, Edmund Francis Airey, Sr., helped to generously fund the church construction.) So, the History here feels right to honor my mom today.

When my mom would correct my school papers she would lament, "Matthew, what are you trying to say?"

My friend Hank asked me last week, "Buddy, have ya had a good cry yet." I replied, "Brother, I don't think so, but know that I have been crying for the last 7 years about my mom. And have being thinking long about what I would say today."

So, mom, this is what I am trying to say with a sense of History. Humor. And Love. I want to talk about:

1. Gratitude

2. Formation

3. Legacy

In expressing my mom's Gratitude today, I admit:

My words are poor, but my thankful memories rich.

My sorrows are deep, but all of your kindness fulfilling.

My capacities are limited, but her gratitude endless.

Regina Marie Airey. Gina Bina from Pasadena. Gin. You have certainly come a long way, from almost being born in the front seat of a 1956 Ford. In 1981, when my sister needed lifesaving surgery, my mom was my sisters' advocate. My mom directly told the doctors, "You take care of my daughter and keep her healthy."

Gina showed her gratitude toward my mom by becoming her constant advocate. Gina and I would meet with countless doctors and nurses, and when they would look toward me, and I would smile to indicate ... "I relinquish my time to the senator from California," meaning, the bulldog was in action.

Gina got my mom healthy in 2013 before her open-heart surgery. Gina advocated for mom to receive more physical therapy, time after time. And she would appeal short hospital stays. Words cannot express our gratitude.

Gina experienced the joy of travel with my mom and dad, and just with the two of them to the South Pacific. Those two vagabonds shared the delight of countless musicals, plays and movies intimately until my mom's last breath. Thank you. I truly appreciate your generous spirit with our mother; and all while we were trying to raise three active sons.

My wife, Christy, her daughter in law, whom she loved. Christy, who allowed my mom to become Nana, when Garrett, Shane and Connor were born.

On January 3, 2020, my mom was rushed to the emergency room. A respiration mask was placed over mom's mouth. Mom was pretty much unconscious. Christy went up to her and said, "Hello Nana, we are here." My mom replied through her mask. "Hello sweetie." Powerful. I didn't get a 'Hello Sweetie,' but Christy did.

The relationship with a daughter-in-law, and a mother in law is sometimes unique. By the way, my favorite mother in law is here, so I have a reference. One time, I called my mom after the boys were at her house after school. I asked, "How did it go?" My mom complained that the boys (probably Garrett) were reading the expiration dates on chips and crackers and said they couldn't eat them. Mom questioned me, "Did your wife, teach them that?"

There were incredible times with Nana at sporting and school events. Shane and Connor would do crafts and paint coffee mugs and bowls and go to lunch.

My mom and dad would come over to our first home for trick-or-treating. My dad would give out the candy. And the rest of us would walk through the neighborhood. My mom's favorite Halloween story was when Garrett was Captain Hook, Shane was Peter Pan, of course. And CJ (Connor) was the Crocodile with a long thick tail. Mom was pushing Connor in the stroller, and she rolled over his tail. She started to hear Connor's faint voice grow stronger, "Nana My Tail, Nana My Tail."

In 1989 when Pape Jim died, the brother, my Uncle George, and sister had to work out the affairs and money. I would hear them on the phone and detected a caring and practical exchange. I distinctly remember thinking that this is the way Gina and I need to work together. Thank you.

My Aunt Judy called my mom Marg. Judy got my grandparent's marriage blessed in the early 1960s. God bless her. The background story here is that Judy was my mother's sister-in-law and was married to George Gerberick. My mother's parents, Jim, and Josephine Gerberick were not married in the Catholic Church in 1930, because the Italian Catholic priest did not approve that Jim was German and not a Catholic. So, the couple had a simple civil service. Jim supported Josephine's faith by driving her to Mass and by teaching the faith to their children. These actions helped Judy to arrange for Jim and Josephine to finally get married in the Catholic Church. The Catholic Church law requires baptized Roman Catholics like Josephine to marry before a priest or deacon. Catholics who exchange vows in the presence of ministers from other religious traditions or civil officials are not considered validly married in the eyes of the Catholic Church. I know Judy's act of kindness meant a lot to my grandmother and my mom.

God's generosity can't be outdone, but the following individuals came very close. Thanks. My cousins, Audine, Amanda, Terry, Jim. You were totally dedicated to Auntie Rite. You have been an unbelievable rock of humor and love.

One time at Saint Jude's before my mom went into surgery for a "pick line," we were all in the pre-op area laughing and talking loudly. And the nurses said, "Please kept it down or you will have to leave."

To Our Angles. Angelica. Cindi. Lupe. Ana. Sandra. Sylvia. God's Blessings to you and your families. These fine people were my mother's 24x7 home caregivers.

To the Saint Denis Eucharistic Ministers, and especially to Jack and Rose. Your sense of the duty and evangelization is a blessing. The ministers would call me on a Saturday or a Sunday and ask when they could see Marguerite. My sarcastic reply, "Geez, that's so tough, she has such a demanding schedule. Any time after 11 a.m." Just so you know, my mom broke her hip when she was answering the door for the Eucharistic Ministers. Jack, I won't send you the bill.

My mom is so grateful for, as I am, for her Grandparents, the Gerbericks and Termines.

And all of the Termine aunts and uncles, and cousins:
Uncle Sam,
Aunt Tootsie (Victoria), Uncle Merle, Paulette, Skip, Chuck,
Uncle Vic, Aunt Alice, David, Gibb,
Uncle Joe,
Aunt Catherine, Uncle Nuke, Greg, Nancy.

My mom lived with Aunt Catherine (her mom's youngest sister) and Uncle Nuke (Catherine's husband) for a while, when my mom was at San Diego State University. She was close to Aunt Catherine and Uncle Nuke, who lived in the Chula Vista near San Diego and who helped my mom through her college years. When I was a young boy, mom, Gina and I took the train in the summertime to San Diego to visit Aunt Catherine and Uncle Nuke. One time, I asked Aunt Catherine, if I could have something else to eat soon after we finished breakfast.

"Matthew, the kitchen is closed."

My mom gave me the "knock it off signal."

The Aireys. My dad loved his wife and was so grateful for her care and companionship. My mom told me that very early in their courtship, like the second or third date. My dad insisted that they visit his family at the Airey Ranch. My mom was reluctant, and she soon found a ton of people there, very active and loud, probably some Engh kids (the kids from my dad's oldest sister) running around. But she was ok, her comfort level increased. Papa Ed nicknamed mom, Margo. Margo loved all of you. Four years ago, my cousin, Steve Engh, mentioned to me that mom was a die-hard with well wishes and Mass cards and letters.

The Abbotts. To all of you. Thank you. My brother-in-law, David Baiza's, recent voice mail said it best, "She was a fantastic woman, ever since I met her."

Bishop Amat brothers and sisters. I love you. You're certainly steadfast, loyal and true. My mom wrote and read a poem with all of the players' names from our Amat sophomore football team. I think it was published in our yearbook.

Jimmy fondly reminisced, when we would come to my home late at night, but my mom was still up. I was tired, so I went to bed, but my mom and Jimmy stayed up to watch David Letterman, Saturday Night Live, Johnny Carson. And Linda Ellerbe. My mom enjoyed humorous conversations and stupid fun humor.

Another time, my USC friend, Rob Maywood, and I came home after way too much to drink. After we greeted my mom, we went into the kitchen to get something to eat. Rob observed that there was a wide assortment of vegetables and fruits in the kitchen. You know, my dad was an active participant at the farmers market. In Rob's state of frivolity, he focused on and pointed to the oversized "Beef Steak Tomatoes." And we could not stop laughing. My mom came into the kitchen, assessed the silliness, and laughed along with us.

Formation

My mom absolutely adored her parents. And they were critical to my mother's formation, in all aspects of her life.

Here's what my close Servite priest friend, Don Duplessie told with me when I shared my grandmother's family background. My Nana, Josephine, was born to Sicilian immigrants near New Orleans. Father Don mentioned that his family was from New Orleans and were French immigrants. He noted the Italians faced severe discrimination. "Matt, you come from very humble beginnings."

My mom shared that my Nana Josephine took in laundry, ironing and sewing to make extra money. My mom was crushed (as we were) when her mother died at just 62 years old in 1972.

Mom's faith formation was shaped, in part, by her cousin, Marjorie Benjamin, who took her to church and showed mom the missal and hymns. My mom told me, "A void was filled in my life even as a young girl by learning more about the Church."

Also, her Confirmation sponsor was Lee Alfano (another Italian), who supported her formation. Lee called mom "Marge," and the two of them became fellow All Souls Church (Alhambra, California) catechism teachers and lifelong friends.

About six years ago, I was on one of my daily driving home, after work calls with my mom, and she shared a very emotional story about her dad. And my mom had a casual but meaningful purpose to her memories. She told me that after she secured her teaching job at Temple City High School in 1956, she informed her dad that she would once again work during the summer as a park recreation supervisor (Pasadena, California). Her dad, Papa Jim, said, "No. You're a professional now, so you don't need to work in the summer. If you need anything, your mother and I will provide it." I was overcome with emotion, because of papa's kindness and support of my mother. So, I lied to my mom. "Mom, sorry, got to go and take this work call." I was weeping so hard after hearing this memory that I had to pull off to the side of the road. The love my mother experienced from her parents continue through her to her children.

My mom's formation of me.

My mom was tough, but always encouraging and loving toward me with school, sports, and my life. Treat others with respect, especially if they are way younger or older than you. Mom could be direct too, "Thirteen hours of labor for you. I gave you my ticket to see Pope John Paul the Second."

During elementary school, my mom noticed that I was having a tough time memorizing:

"The Song of Hiawatha." "You know Matthew, I was a teacher, and I also know Native American Hand Signals." Mom started to motion her hands in various ways.

By the shore of Gitche Gumee,

By the shining Big-Sea-Water,

At the doorway of his wigwam,

She started to laugh. She really got me on that one.

<u>No Irish Need Apply.</u>

My mom would go out her way for us to celebrate Saint Patrick's Day. She would make wonderful corned beef, cabbage, potatoes, and shepherd's pie. In later years, the two of us would always celebrate the holiday at a local restaurant, and I would make sure mom felt no pain after her two green Mojitos or various rum drinks.

After mom rehabilitated from her hip surgery, she was discharged from her facility on March 17, 2017. But the show must go on. Shaney picked up the corned beef and shepherds' pie from the Yardhouse, and the Duffys arrived for the celebration. A toast. Slainte. Mission accomplished.

My affection for popular music came from my mom, who would have the radio on in the house. Early on, we were watching late night movies on TV during the summer. Elvis. I was hooked. My 1970 birthday gift was an 8 Track Tape from my mom with our personally selected favorites: The Who, Credence Clearwater Revival, Bobby Sherman, Five Stairsteps, Tom Jones, and the Friends of Distinction song ..."Grazing in the grass is a gas, baby can you dig it?" Just saying it makes ya feel good.

(Note: Song Title Tracks Included: "Hitchin' A Ride," "Silver Bird," "Wigwam," "Easy Come Easy Go," "Down on the Corner," "Light My Fire," "Little Woman," "Working on a Groovy Thing," "Proud Mary," "Overture from Tommy," "Grazing in the Grass," "I'm Gonna Make You Love Me," "It's Not Unusual," "O-o-h Child," "Sweet Caroline.")

Together we would pray to her Favorite Italian Saints: Francis, Anthony, and Padre Pio. And finally, Saint Jude, 'The Patron Saint of the Impossible'. Saint Therese. Our Lady of Lourdes.

But for me the most profound formation for my mom may have been the day before her 2013 open heart surgery at Mission Hospital (Mission Viejo, California). The priest motioned mom and I into a small medical room and quietly closed the door. He anointed her with the Sacrament of the Sick. The priest then raised his hands and gave my mom absolution. A euphoric sense of peace and confidence "reigned over me." Mission accomplished once again. Heaven.

Legacy.

Now, I will attempt to be my mother's voice regarding her Legacy by sharing these thoughts. In July 1969, I was sitting on the cool linoleum floor during summer school at Ybarra Elementary (Rowland Heights, California). They showed us a black and white film of a young man saying, "We choose to go to the moon, not because it is easy, but because it is hard."

When I got home, I told my mom about the film, and asked who the man was. "Matt that was President John F. Kennedy. He was Catholic and Irish, just like you." Wow, that sounded encouraging. "Mom, what happened to him?" "They killed him." Remember my mom could be direct; especially with me.

President Kennedy noted, "When my great-grandfather came to America, he carried nothing with him except two things – A strong religious faith and a strong desire for liberty." This was such the case of my ancestors and that of most Americans. We are a nation of Immigrants. As I tell my sons. The only reason you're here, is because someone decided to get on boat.

On another day during my youth, my mom showed me a new bracelet she bought. The bracelet was a simple aluminum band with a man's name on it and the words: Captain J. Clifford McKittrick. 6 – 16 – 67. United States Army. Missing in Action. Vietnam. (Note: I proudly have this bracelet in my possession.)

Who does that kind of thing? My mother did. She had a worldly, considerate, and concerned view of life.

Finally, I wholehearted believe that my mother would base her own legacy on

- History,
- Her Gratitude,
- and Her Faith Formation.

And the kindness she shared with all.

I have cherishing love and thankfulness for my mother's caring and love for me.

And within that spirit, I share the following hopeful and timely message with you, and especially with:

Garrett Matthew

Shane Abbott

Connor James

Senator Robert F. Kennedy. Indianapolis, Indiana. April 4, 1968. (Not full text of speech.)

Introduction: I believe in my mind and heart that Senator Robert F. Kennedy eloquently and sincerely articulated my mother's view of American in 1968 and for America's long-term progression. She believed that advancement must contain compassion and collaboration. I also chose to share key aspects of Senator's Kennedy's speech regarding the death of Dr. Martin Luther King, because two days after me after my mother's funeral, America celebrated Martin Luther King Day on Monday, January 20, 2020. I felt the present moment required acute awareness of our history and their direct relevance to our nation's current challenges, and of course, to my mother's perspective.

Senator Kennedy began ...

I have bad news for you, for all of our fellow citizens, and people who love peace all over the world, and that is that Martin Luther King was shot and killed tonight.

Dr. King dedicated his life to love and to justice for his fellow human beings, and he died because of that effort.

In this difficult day, in this difficult time for the United States, it is perhaps well to ask what kind of a nation we are
and what direction we want to move in.

We can make an effort, as Dr. King did, to understand and to comprehend,
and to replace that violence, that stain of bloodshed that has spread across our land,
with an effort to understand with compassion and love.

What we need in the United States is not division;
what we need in the United States is not hatred;
what we need in the United States is not violence or lawlessness;
but love and wisdom,
and compassion toward one another,
and a feeling of justice toward those who still suffer within our country,

So, I shall ask you tonight to return home,
to say a prayer for the family of Dr. King,
but more importantly to say a prayer for our own country,
which all of us love—a prayer for understanding and that compassion of which I spoke.

Note: The Monday following my mother's funeral was Martin Luther King Day, January 20, 2020.

Your Life's Takeaways:

Reflect on a loved one's Gratitude (living or passed on). How did your loved one show their gratitude? ____.

What are you currently grateful for? ____.

How is your gratitude expressed? ____.

Who was critical in forming / influencing your loved one's life?

What three experiences made you the person you are?

What three experiences inspire you to be the best version of yourself?

What is your current legacy? ____.

What do you need to adjust or address within your current legacy? ____.

What do you want your Legacy to be? ____.

Chapter 7: "I'm The Quarterback."

Introduction: US Navy Commander William Joseph "Bill" Gault. July 19, 1954 – February 28, 2019.

A key catalyst to finish my book was the death of my true friend, Bill, from bladder cancer. The following pages are my reflective memories that I shared with Bill's wife, son, and sister. It forced me to become steadfastly aware and write some profound life's takeaways due to my shock, sorrow, gratitude, and joy.

In Memory of US Navy Commander William Joseph "Bill" Gault. 1954 - 2019

Beloved husband of Denise D'Onofrio Gault. Dear Father of William Michael Gault "Billy". Brother of the late Don Gault and Beth Gault Hoffmiester (Jim A. Hoffmiester). Retired Commander US Navy Supply Corps. Passed away at the age of 64 on Thursday, February 28, 2019 after a long and courageous battle with bladder cancer.

Bill was born on July 19, 1954 in Brownsville, Pennsylvania to the late Shirley F. Gault and late William M. Gault and grew up in Parma, Ohio. After graduating from Baldwin-Wallace College in 1976, Bill entered the Navy on September 24 of that same year. During his Navy service from 1976 to 1998 his afloat assignments included Assistant to the Supply Officer on the destroyer USS Newman K Perry (DD-883), Assistant to the Supply Officer and commissioning crew member of the Submarine tender USS McKee (AS-41), and Supply Officer on the guided missile cruiser USS Reeves (CG-24). His shore assignments include Contracting training in Washington, D.C., Supply officer assignments for the Seabees, Marines and Pacific Fleet Submarine force. While on active duty CDR Gault earned his MBA from San Diego State

University. After retiring from the Navy, Bill joined Lockheed Martin Corp. until his retirement in 2013.

Bill was an amazing and devoted husband and father. A wonderful man who led by example. His greatest joy was being with his family. Music was a big part of his life whether it was listening to Maynard Ferguson blast the trumpet, attending numerous concerts with Denise and Billy, and playing the drums at home. A sports enthusiast, runner and avid golfer he was always very active and competitive. He enjoyed watching sports, especially on the sidelines at Billy's track meets, basketball, flag football, and soccer games. He taught Billy what it is to be a loyal sports fan as he cheered on his Bears, Indians and Cavs in victory and defeat. He looked forward to selecting his picks with Billy during March Madness and most recently had fun learning the workings of Fantasy Football from Billy. His infectious laugh and great personality invited everyone in. He cared first about how you were before his own needs. He left Billy with some thoughts to always remember "Do your best, always work hard, do what's right, and treat others as you want to be treated". He was loved to the fullest and will be forever missed.

Bill's Funeral Mass held on Tuesday, March 19, 2019 at 10 AM at Saint Mary Magdalene, 1945 Illion Street, San Diego, CA 92110

Bill is buried at Miramar National Cemetery, 5795 Nobel Drive, San Diego, CA 92122.

Denise. Billy. Beth.

I believe in redemptive suffering and redemptive salvation, and Bill is enjoying eternal peace in Heaven. Denise, Billy, Beth and the extended Gault family and friends actively participated in this event of redemption suffering during the last seven or so years with Bill's battle with cancer.

The Mother Teresa Center (motherteresa.org) posted the following on redemption suffering:

> "You'll find that it is not uncommon to hear one Catholic tell another who is suffering to "offer it up" as a way of dealing with his suffering. It should be remembered, though, that while it is most definitely good to tell someone to "offer it up," it is also easy — and that we are called, too, to comfort those who are suffering, to feed the hungry, to give drink to the thirsty, to care for the sick, etc. Telling someone to offer it up without also helping him to deal with the temporal and emotional effects of whatever they are going through is not the fully Christian thing to do. Even Our Lord was helped while carrying His Cross: St. Veronica wiped the sweat and Blood from His Holy Face, and St. Simon of Cyrene helped Him bear the Cross itself."

Commander Gault fought the good fight every step of the way. And through his baptism and being a strong man, a strong man as a husband, a strong man as a father, he is reaping these blessed benefits by possessing such qualities. Bill is there in heaven playing ball with all his old shipmates and his brother Don, while seeing his mom and dad and countless others who loved him.

I wanted to share a few stories of my friendship with Bill for which I'm eternally grateful and humbled.

Here we go. I met Bill Gault in September 1985 at San Diego State University Master of Business Administration class, business law. I can remember in the first day class, and it was within a "tiered stepped classroom" setting with about three or four levels. Bill was on about the third level, and I was on second level. I came in and sat down catty corner in front of him. During the first-class break, I turned around and saw Billy smiled at me. He said, "I am Bill Gault," and extended his hand. I extended my hand back, shock his hand, and said, "Hi. I'm Matt Airey."

I asked Bill, "So what are you doing here?"

He said he was in the Navy, and the Navy paid for his education. My inside voice started to wonder, that sounds like a pretty good deal and there's no way in hell this guy looks like a naval officer. I'm always been kind of critical of people. I'm working on my faults, but in this sense, it was all good-natured. Bill and I continued some chitchat small talk. Then he told me about the MBA graduate students' men's flag football team, and that they played on Saturdays.

"So okay," I said. "I played very competitive high school football and rugby in college."

"Let me ask you a question. So, who's the quarterback?"

Bill said, "I am the quarterback." My inside voice said, you're s***ing me.

Wow, this really got my interest up. This was just not computing for me. Bill did not appear to me to be quarterback, let alone a football player, although he was over 6 feet tall and lanky and wiry and muscular. I just didn't see the prowess on the gridiron for him, but we would have to see what would unfold. I agreed to meet Bill and the guys on Friday to start a practice.

I have a lot of pride in playing the game of football, so I recruited a few players. Namely, one of my best friends from high school who was at San Diego State, Hank "Mad Dog" Arellano. I also recruited another one of my classmates, David Kreiman. The first thing we needed to do is have a line that could protect the quarterback. And to defensively rush the opposing quarterback to have any chance of competing; let alone winning. But we would surely be up against it; along with our advanced years maybe just two or three years older than normal students that were playing. Bill had eight years on me .... an old man roughly 30 years old with the pigskin in his hand.

Football is my favorite sport, and I coached kids in South Central Los Angeles. I had a part time job during my freshman year in college coaching young junior high school students in flag football. All of the young teenage men were African American. What a joyful growth experience for the players and me. We helped each other to be patient and supportive, and we won a ton of football games.

This was a formidable experience in my youth. I was only 18 years old, and I was permitted to lead, teach, and coach these young men. Today, I would not have been permitted to have this opportunity without a complete background check, extensive legal paperwork, and being over 21 years old. I was supervised and had to complete status reports, but I definitively had to rely on my skills, quick wit, and determination to share the discipline and excitement of playing football.

During one of our first practices, I found it productive to spread the players out on the field, while I explained the role of each offensive and defensive position. I repeated this process and began to slowly walk through the plays versus just playing sandlot touch football. It was difficult for my players to focus, since they did not have previous organized sports experience

This difficultly was exemplified once when a neighborhood kid started to walk near our practice with a brown bag filled with hot greasy French fries. My players immediately left the drill and grabbed some fries from the kid. I was pissed. But then I started to laugh hysterically at myself and the situation, and so did my players once they saw me. I think it was God's humorous way to telling me I am not fully in charge. I needed to be more patient with myself and others. Heck, I love hot fries too. I let them finish the fries; then we got back to the drill.

I soon became more aware that these young African American men lived in a different world from my background. I would sometimes drop them off at their homes after late afternoon practice. Some players were gracious enough to invite me in to meet their parents, grandparents, aunts, and uncles. I felt honored that the players, and hopefully their family, trusted me. I enjoyed introducing myself and shaking their hands. Although I was focused on properly presenting myself to the adults, I could not help but noticed many homes lacked carpet, furniture, and painted walls. Many of the players lived with extended family members in houses that had little tender loving care since the 1950s and 1960s. I was learning about life and the lives of those I encountered. I certainly was not very wise at a young age, but I tried not to avoid learning about my players. I was hopeful that these young men could do well in school and live full, productive, and joyous lives, while facing the economic challenges facing them. Many financial obstacles remain for people of color in the United States, but white Americans are often unaware of such circumstances. Many people do not have personal references involving an uneven playing field that includes challenging criminal justice system. Some of us may harbor unfounded fear of the unknown – people who are different.

I affectionately remember my merry experience with my players when we played our first men's flag football game came. I was playing right guard, David at center, and Hank at left guard. Bill was quarterback. Phil as a wing receiver. Jerry as another receiver. And another two guys to make seven positions: seven on seven. Surprisingly during our final possession, we are able to march down the field and got down to the 15-yard line; in the red zone trying to score. Bill shouted "hut" and then clinched the ball in his hands. He stepped back, and he scrambled to his right. I was blocking the defender. Bill shuffled to his right again and then silence. I couldn't see anything, but I could feel "the sling the ball out of his hand" and whisk past my right ear. The football spiraled to the right corner of the end zone where our receiver friend Phil was headed for the corner pylon. Bill's throw angled low to the front corner of the end zone. Phil extended his hands, got his hands on the ball bullet and touched his feet down. Boom. Touchdown. We win the game. After that great catch, I nicknamed Phil "Sure Hands."

I then turned around and looked at Bill and said, "What the f*** was that s***! You think you're Broadway Joe Willie Namath back, there don't you?" Bill had the widest grin on his face. He appreciated my colorful language and my accolades. It was the start of something magical.

Bill was very competitive on the football field as we were starting to develop plays and rhythms to get him to be able to sling the ball downfield. I also designed a play where Bill threw a screen pass to me on the right for a potential 35-yard gain or a touchdown. Although I was a little bigger than the younger competitors, I still had some quick feet, not fast, but quick. That was my favorite play when I saw the football spiral from Bill to me. Then, I trotted down the field into the end zone. We were extremely competitive.

Bill did not play defense. You can't risk your quarterback getting hurt. We let Bill play some cornerback sometimes, but he just didn't have a feel for the opposite side of the ball. Of course, my friend Hank and I rushed the opposing quarterbacks like "mad dogs."

My nickname was "the Mattress," from one of our classmates, Gil, who described one of my tackles when I fell on top of a ball carrier. Point of reference, you're not supposed to tackle in flag football. I must has missed reading this rule. Wink, wink.

Lastly, sometimes Bill got sacked. His was flag pulled, ball down at that spot. Of course, us lineman blamed Bill for his old slow feet. Ya can't block a rusher forever. "Geez, Bill. Can you f***in' move?" Man, Bill did not like the criticism, and he would mumble something under his breath back to us. If I remember correctly, it was a biological reference to close some parts of our anatomy, and then cease to continue our lives. As previously stated, we were competitive.

Our flag football team played two seasons over the two years. At the end of the second year, we came in sixth out of more than 150 teams. That was a most enjoyable feat, and I must say we enjoyed the after game-celebrations. We extended our flag football success to incorporate the women in our class. As a co-ed team, we became known as the Liquidators.

At the time in the mid-1980s, there was major economic strife the United States - slow growth declining revenues and profits. Some businesses going out of business would have to liquidate their assets to pay off creditors. So, we used the current business phase as a pun, the Liquidators, to establish our prowess in the business community, as well as at local watering holes.

We also played men's and coed softball. Bill played first base, because he had a first baseman's mitt. No, he was asked to play there. Bill was a left-handed batter, so he faced the batter with his right shoulder versus your left shoulder. Bill's big softball claim to fame was in our last coed summer softball championship game (August 16, 1986) played on a field with "a short porch right field fence."

Bill hit two ground ruled doubles over the fence, which hit in runs. I still made fun of Bill from the dugout taunting him that he couldn't pull the softball over the fence. Bill would giggle at the plate, and then turn and whisper some very choice technical words for me under his breath. I think you all saw the picture of that memorable fun day. We did have a good time at the watering hole after that for a bit.

Let me go back to our business law class in the fall (September, October, and November) of 1985. Bill and I decided to study together for a big midterm, so we did the natural thing you need to do when you study; you need to eat. So, we bought two big slabs of meat steak and cooked them on Bill's condo barbecue. I told Bill that I was a meat and potatoes man; so, let's have some potatoes. Bill said I'll make some potatoes for you. I said great. Bill then opened up a box of Betty Crocker Spuds. These are mashed potatoes that you make with water. In my book, this was not a potato, but we had to work with what we had. So, after I gave him some crap about not being able to produce "real potatoes" with our meat slabs, he did proceed to make some very delicious mashed potatoes. And I think Bill did have some margarine we could put on the spuds, along with some salt and pepper.

As we were eating our slabs, all of a sudden, we heard a pop pop pop. In Bill's high voice he exclaimed. "What was that?" I looked at Bill, and I said "Bill, those were gunshots. Go call 911." I ran down downstairs through the back-stairwell underneath Bill's second story condo. I could hear someone outside the back-metal door pounding loudly, bang bang bang. "Let me in! Let me in!" I opened the door towards the outside and there was a middle-aged man there clutching his gut. The man said, "I been shot. I've been shot." So, I pulled him towards me and embraced him in a bear hug and brought the man inside the stairwell. I slammed the door shut and knelt down on the ground. When I opened up the man's shirt, I could see a black hole about the size of a penny with blood gushing out of it. I had blood on my hands.

Bill rushed downstairs and said, "Matt, what the f*** is going on?" I said, "Billy, this guy's been shot. Go get me some towels, so I can put pressure on his wound." Bill raced back upstairs and brought down two blue towels that quickly absorbed the blood as I put pressure on the man's wound. Bill went back upstairs to take the phone call from the police and monitor the situation. Just about that time within about three minutes or so, there were more big banging sounds on the metal door, bang bang bang. "San Diego Police. Let us in. Let us in." I put my last pressure on the gentleman's stomach where the blood was, and I got up to answer the door. When I answered the door, I had three police guns pointed at me and one officer politely said, "Who the f*** are you?"

The police quickly escorted me out of the building and into a squad car in the backseat near the parked cars near the first floor. They asked for my ID, and I complied. In the meantime, Bill came back down the stairs; I was told. As the police officers and soon the paramedics tended to aid the shot gentleman, I waited in the squad car for what seemed like at least 20 minutes. Eventually during that time, I saw Bill outside talking to the officers as well. I understand how the police maneuver and how they question people so they can compare stories; so, I was prepared to tell the truth since I nothing to hide. The police went through their series of questions, "If I knew the man? If I knew what happened? If he said anything etc. etc.?" I said, "No, we were just upstairs, eating slabs of meat and homemade mashed potatoes; and all of a sudden we heard gunshots." The Commanding Police officer asked me why I knew those were gunshots. I said, "I went to school at USC near South Central Los Angeles, and I used to hear gun shots all the time." A sad reality of life in that period of time.

The police released me, and Bill and I went back to studying. I must tell you it was pretty shaky to have that type of experience and actually see someone who nearly died right in front of me. Apparently, two men came up to this man and shot him, because he wouldn't hand over his keys. In those days carjacking was a new thing. This man, I guess had a new sports car, I think it was a Porsche, and there was no way in hell he was going to give it up. Maybe not the greatest decision he ever made, since a car can be replaced.

Fast forward to the 1986 NFL NFC playoffs, my favorite, Los Angeles Rams, versus Bill's favorite, the Chicago Bears. The Bears were a powerhouse and very confident and even recorded a music video called the Super Bowl Shuffle. It was a cold snowy day in Chicago for the game, and the visiting Rams were not as adept to that weather. Bill was out of town that weekend, but I knew he was watching the game just like me. The Rams took it on the chin that game and once again number 34 "Sweetness" Walter Payton and their awesome 46 defense took care of business. Bears defensive coordinator Buddy Ryan named his defense the "46 defense" after Doug Plank's jersey number and his central position (safety position) in the defense. Doug Plank had a hard hitting and aggressive style, which Coach Ryan favored. The Bears were headed to the Super Bowl.

We watched that Super Bowl with a collection of friends at Bill's condo in January 1986. The Bears had the game under control during the first half. So, at half time, we went downstairs to throw the pigskin around. In those days, the Super Bowl halftime shows were not as big a production as they are now, with minimal corporate sponsorship and marginal acts with a few exceptions.

As we threw around the football at half time, a middle-aged man and his wife walked up to Bill, and then they motioned for me to come over to them. It appeared from Bill's expression and within my returned expression that we did not know who these mystery people were. But we were soon to find out.

The woman touched my forearm said, "You saved my husband's life. You saved my husband's life, you did."

I said, "No ma'am, but thank you very much. It's good that it all worked out for you."

The women disagreed, "Yes you did. You two were at the right place at the right time!" Bill and I just looked at each other with a silent glance on our faces. We took that moment in seriously.

I think Bill and I had a full appreciation of life even at a young age, and we looked forward to life in the fullest. We were young smart people, trying to get smarter and trying to make our way in the changing world order. It was a tough economy with high unemployment and high interest rates. So, it felt good to appreciate the simpler things in life; family, new friends, football; and just everyday life. Together, Bill and I made that moment happen.

During this time in San Diego, Bill had some medical complications from some scarring in his urinary track. I don't mean to get too personal or disrespectful by telling you this story, but it has a very poignant experience regarding the character of Bill. I went to several of the appointments with Bill, and since I was a male I could attend. In the end, Bill had a successful surgery and was later placed in the Naval Hospital. (I believe it was in Balboa Park near downtown San Diego).

I went to visit Bill a couple of times there, and one time pulled me aside to one of the sides of his bed. He started to whisper and began talking about one naval patient, who was near Bill's location. This showed me one of the many incredible character traits of Bill. Bill described that the patient next to him was suffering from cancer, probably terminal cancer. The patient was married and had two kids. Bill was astounded at the patient's fate. Bill demonstrated, as he always did, a more silent humility and a deep appreciation for others. His compassion for others and his awareness of his surroundings was unmistakable. Even though Bill may not have said anything about his concern or wrote anything about it, Bill was always aware of the people around him and demonstrated profound care and compassion.

Let me share another recent story with you. I was at the Los Angeles Memorial Coliseum at the Notre Dame versus USC Trojans game in November 2018. I've been fortunate to attend many of the great college football rivalry games between Norte Dame and USC. I watched all them on TV growing up as a little kid; just like Bill did. Just before kickoff, I texted Bill a picture of myself, my son Garrett, my son Connor, and their friend, Sam. In return to the text, Bill sent a picture of his dad who graduated from USC in 1947. Bill's dad was a World War II veteran who went to college like millions of others in that era on the G.I. Bill. Thousands of the veterans went to USC. The picture is of Bill's dad in his black cap and gown in a black and white picture facing the West. And the photo shows in the East, the parastall of the Los Angeles Memorial Coliseum and the clock and the temperature gauge. A classic worldwide venue.

Bill absolutely adored his mother and his father was respectful to them, and he told them how much he loved them. That was very evident. Bill was very concerned for and consoling toward his brother, Don. Don came out in 1986 for a little bit; let's say gap year to sort a few things out. Bill welcomed Don into his home with no questions asked. His sister, Beth, who he adored spent many days in San Diego with us on pleasure and business trips. Bill loved and

67

respected his family and his humble Midwestern beginnings in Parma, Ohio. And he much appreciated his opportunity to be on the West Coast and to serve his country in the Navy.

Here's another fun story. In 1987, we are on spring break but many of our friends left the San Diego area to go home for a visit. One spring day found just Bill, me and my friend, Angie Ojeda, who drove down from LA to San Diego alone. Bill asked in his high-pitched voice, "What are we gonna do?" I said, "Well, let's start drinking. Let's go to the beach." So, we got in Angie's car, and we went down to Pacific Beach to a place right on the sand called Lahaina. It reminded Bill of some of his Navy days in the Hawaiian Islands (Lahaina is on Maui). This place was a simple bar with the porch that goes out to the sand, and we started drinking pitchers of beer. For you younger people who read this; it was root beer. It was a beautiful San Diego clear beach day. Totally Awesome (1980s slang). We just sat and talked and met a few people. We even got the bartender to put on some Rolling Stones, my favorite band, so we could pump up the vibe a little more.

Needless to say, after some drinking; we were meeting our limit pretty fast. "I'm hungry," Bill said. "Let's get something to eat." I said, "That's great. Let's go to that Italian place by school." Bill said, "No, I gotta go and meet this girl I'm dating." I said, "Bill that's bull s***! You're not gonna go to see a girl after we've been drinking. We're gonna go to the Italian place and have some calzone, and that's that." Bill reluctantly agreed, but he had one condition. He said, "I gotta call her that I won't make it and will have to re-schedule." I said, "Fine, you can call her from the restaurant later. Don't worry about it."

We arrived at the Italian place, we ordered a calzone and some other Italian food; probably something else more to drink too. Bill went to the payphone. Remember, no cell phones at the time. Nobody knew where you are at. No pagers. No nothing, you had the rendezvous by using the phone and plan ahead (where to meet and when). As Bill was on the phone trying to sweet talk this gal, I could tell he was having a rough time. So of course, as one of his best buddies; Matt decided intervening. I don't know if I asked for the phone; I probably just ripped it out of his hands (remember lots of root beer). But Bill had a big grin and laughed about my strategy. Let's just say my un-sober negotiating skills are probably not as effective as my sober negotiating skills. The girl on the other side quickly hung up on me. But before she did, she told me that she was pissed off and this was all my fault. "It's your fault Matt Airey. You did this to Bill." Guilty as charged, but what a great time. We had another great fun time. After a couple days went by, Bill finally saw the girl, and I saw the girl too. Of course, my profuse apology was "totally sincere." Wink, wink.

Fast forward to when I was visiting New York while working for IBM (1998 – 2001). I got in touch with Bill, who I believe was in New Jersey at the time doing some contract work. Bill and I rendezvoused to go out to dinner, and, of course, the menu would be slabs and real potatoes, this time. Since I had my IBM expense account, I gladly paid for the lavish dinner at Ruth Chris Steak House. Just like old times, two guys having a slab and potatoes; no shooting this time, just a great visit. We decided to go back to the hotel and continue our conversation.

Bill mentioned that he met a new woman, he was really keen on and her name was Denise. He told me that she was an attorney. I shared that he better be careful during his courting negotiations with Denise. Bill enjoyed the "ribbing" and laughed. Bill continued that Denise was Italian. My reply was perfect. I said I will just ask you one more question, "Is she Catholic?" "Yes," Bill reluctantly replied. "I love this. I told you that we would finally get to you. The Catholics would bring you into the fold," I boasted. I can't repeat what Bill told me, but it was some very fine technical language that we used to exchange with another.

I was once again prodding my true friend, who was smitten with this new woman. I said, "Bill, I have quite a successful track record of the negotiating for you with women. Let me call her up now." "No f***ing way you're calling this one, Matt. I really like her." That was so damn funny. I knew that Bill was very serious about his sweetheart, and that his heart and his mind we're aligned to love Denise.

I'm now going to try to summarize what this person of Bill Gault meant to me. But here it goes. I'm a very loyal person. I'm not perfect; but I'm loyal to Bill as he was always loyal to me. Even though there were gaps in our communication because of family, travel, and jobs, Bill was always loyal. We would write each other letters, we would talk on the phone, and we both appreciated that proactive type of friendship, tradition, and commitment.

Bill was an exceptional audience for me. He would laugh at my jokes. He would push back at me with fun, but Bill would also challenge me. What else could a man ask for in a true friend? I don't think much more. I remember another time about Bill's loyalty, when just the two of us we went out to Mission Beach. We stumbled across a recording studio where you could pay $15 and record a karaoke song in the sound booth. Bill prodded me to record Elvis, my number one favorite artist, and he offered to pay. I went in and sang "Don't Be Cruel." Bill stood outside as people walked by and listened to the outside speakers. He was like the Circus Barker calling people near to listen. We had my voice and the music track recorded on a cassette tape. Sorry to say, I cannot find the tape, but it does not matter because I have those sweet memories - another recorded Elvis song. Man, I really appreciate Bill's support always. We had a lot of fun.

Bill slung the football like Broadway Joe Willie Namath and served as a Naval Officer for 22 years for his country that he sincerely loved. Bill, husband, a devoted husband, cherished husband so appreciative of his wife and family always. Bill, the dedicated father and a father that knew that his son, Billy, would be successful no matter what. Bill shared with his family the meaning of life that would help them carry on and be successful. These values were repeated in Denise's eulogy, and I'm sure many more of these guidelines remain in our hearts, minds and prayers.

Remember, when God takes something away from us, He gives us the memories to provide us solace. Since we believe in the eternal soul, we have a unique way to communicate daily with the ones that we've lost. Thanks so much for allowing me to share these deep thoughts and feelings and memories. I will never forget them. I know you won't forget either.

God's Speed.

Matthew Edmund Airey. May 19, 2019.

> "If you're not gonna go ALL the way, why go at ALL?"- Broadway Joe Willie Namath, New York Jets.

My dear brother Bill. Thank you for your love, laughter and friendship. I love you. I cherish the memories. Fight On!

I last visited Bill on Saturday, February 23, 2018. After our visit, I gave him and hug and kiss on the forehead before I left, and he started to go to sleep from the morphine. I walked downstairs and started to say my goodbyes to Denise. After a minute, Bill shouted downstairs to me, "Hey Matt. Thanks for comin' huh." Precious.

Your Life's Takeaways:

Be open to meeting new people. You will never know if you just met a potential lifelong friend. List the new people and friends you have currently know. ____.

Remain humble and allow people around you to support and encourage you; you need that assistance more than you know. Have you been humble? ____.

What can you do to improve this trait? ____.

Keep believing in your life's plan. Maybe it is God's Plan, more joy is awaiting. What do you need to do to become more confident in your current life plan? ____.

Be loyal to your true friends and family. They probably will demonstrate their loyalty to you. Who have you been very loyal to? ____.

Who should you be more loyal to in your current life? ____.

A sample of the texts and emails I saved from Bill.

Sad news Matt, I just learned that Mike Grossblatt passed away last Friday after a lengthy battle with brain cancer. He was only 56. You may also hear from Jane. Jane and Beth talk frequently, and Beth let me know. Their son graduates high school in June 2018 and starts college in the fall. Hard to believe. I have so many great memories of Mike. He, like my brother, is gone way too soon. Mike will sure be missed. May God be with his family. Love, Bill

Broadway, I share your heartfelt emotions. Don and Mike can play softball in heaven together and maybe have a few cool ones. Jane sent me an email, and I replied. I forwarded that email to you. God's help to them. Matt

I like your picture of heaven. That would sure work for me! And whiskey would be a welcome addition to this treatment. Have a great day buddy. You're the best! Bill

On Jun 14, 2017, at 8:13 PM, <u>billgault</u> wrote:

> **Hi Matt,**
> **Not sure you're getting my replies to your text, so here they are in e-mail.**
> **All the best,**
> **Bill:**

Broadway. How are you and the family?

Mark your calendar. Sept 2. Qualcomm. UC Davis Connor Airey vs the Aztecs.

Very exciting Mattress! Good for Connor. You and Christy must be thrilled! We're doing alright. I've been back in chemo treatment since February. Finished last week, PET scan this past Monday. Results due by next Monday. How's your mom doing? Love ya pal, Broadway

Bill thinking of you. Your dad. Family today. June 14.

Thanks Matt, you're the best. Some good news, the PET scan results I got Monday showed "no evidence of disease!" So now, I'm done with treatment and back to monitoring. Thank you for your prayers. God has truly blessed us. Love ya buddy, Bill

Today also marks 5 years since my cancer diagnosis. "Fight on"

From: Matthew Airey < >
Date: June 14, 2017 at 9:52:15 PM PDT
To: billgault

Subject: Re: Texts. Airey. Gault.

No evidence of disease ... you mean below the neck. Brother sorry I could not resist. Ha.

Praise God. He answered my prayers for you and the family.

Hope to see you Sept 2 at Connor's game vs Aztecs. We are thrilled. Christy is nervous since Connor hits hard, as a linebacker.

My mom is ok and stable. It's tough brother. My mom lost a lot of cognitive skills, so we have simple conversations. But again, thanks be to God.

Broadway. Kiss the wife and the son for all of us. Fight On!!

Chapter 8: "Mike liked Brunettes. I liked Blonds."

Introduction: Mike Grossblatt succumbed to his battle with brain cancer on Friday March 16, 2018. Like me, Mike was born in 1962, and we attended MBA classes and many events together at San Diego State University from 1985 – 1987. The following pages are my reflective memories that I shared with Mike's wife, Jane, and son, Joe, on April 9, 2018. Meaningful memories should be generously shared with a loved one's family as a simple testimonial of how your life was touched by their family member, along with encouragement for them to Always Move Forward. Sharing a loved one's memories keeps them fresh and alive in our minds and hearts. But more importantly, sharing these memories with a loved one's family provides them with another person's perspective of how their loved one impacted you and possibly varying traits of their loved one's personality. Please try it sometime.

My editor asked me to share more about my relationship with Mike to better understand our closeness. Damn editors always challenging. I do not think I will meet the challenge with spectacular writing. Our relationship was simple. We just got along and really enjoyed each other's company and the moments we had together. Mike and I did not talk a lot, but we "got one another." I was an obnoxious extrovert at times, who danced at bars until I was drenched with sweat. I would come back to the bar table, and Mike would just smile and laugh at me, and ask, "Why'd you stop?" I enjoyed getting a laugh out of him and both of us laughing at each other. When Mike, the quiet introvert danced, he would just slightly step around. We felt comfortable enough with each other and ourselves that we would discuss our pasts, present circumstances, and questions about our future goals. Mike was not a judgmental person, and I sensed he respected me with little regard to my faults. I am very grateful for that.

Jane. Joe.

I am again sending a heartfelt and humble prayer and condolences to you and your family.

I am grateful that you trusted me with this information about my old friend, Mike. I am also very blessed that you and Mike and so many others touched my life.

It has taken me, and of course you, much more time to collect my thoughts and emotions about Mike and our shared experiences.

Joe, you are a young man, and you will conquer your next adventures with the love of your dad, mom, and family. I am sure they imparted much confidence and wisdom upon you. Shocking news makes one reflect, when a person like me and your dad who are just 56 years old, hears of a contemporary's death.

I pray that I am humble enough to appreciate and value life as a precious gift that needs to be shared with others and to support becoming the best version of yourself; and help others to do the same. But moreover, life does not end with our earthly experience, but progresses in the presence of an eternal and all-knowing God. I am reassured that Mike, your dad, is in a heavenly place in peace and without pain, and he will continue to support and guide you and all of us.

One of the comforting phenomena about one's passing are the memories we can immediately recall about them in a warm and cherishing manner. And at times too; these appreciated memories can be humorous.

Honestly, I was thinking of Mike on March 2, 2018 when I visited my friend's dad's condo in La Jolla. My friend's dad bought this place in the fall of 1985. He needed a heavy glass tabletop moved from the street up to his second-floor condo. I conned Mike to help me, but I knew there was money in it for us. And there was ... $50 each. But man, oh man, that damn table was heavy as heck. Mike and I struggled, but together we completed the task. When I saw that table last March, I fondly remembered Mike and our time together.

Mike was intelligent, smart, giving, quiet, focused, stubborn (like me), caring, and intense. He had fun, and I remember him telling me he spent 1984 – 1985 skiing in Colorado after he graduated. "Nice, dude." I reacted. We played flag football at SDSU, and we finished sixth out of 150 teams. Tons of fun. We played softball too. And finally, we played co-ed flag football and softball. We won the summer co-ed softball championship, and Jane was a big contributing athlete in all. These are some of my warmest memories.

Mike and I were just alike....
Mike was Jewish. I was Irish Catholic.
Mike had dark eyes. I had blue eyes.
Mike went to UCLA. I went to USC.
Mike liked Brunettes. I liked Blonds.

Mike and I once drove to Las Vegas in his car, and we stayed with his uncle for free. We drove up from San Diego, and Mike had "prepared a special type of a science project adult beverage... cold, fruity and .... powerful" for our trip. Before we got to Stateline, I told Mike, "I gotta piss." Without a word, Mike quickly pulled off the side of the Highway 15 gravel to an abrupt stop. I looked to my left side, and Mike turned to his right side toward me and did not say a word. I quickly interrupted Mike's undeniable expression. Inside my mind I could hear Mike calmly directed me to get your big ass out of his car and piss. I slightly nodded back and left the vehicle; and accomplished my goal.

I got out of the car and descend down the highway roadside and went to the bathroom. As I returned up the embankment back toward the car, Mike was coming toward me with the similar intention of taking a piss. I smiled back at Mike, and said "What the f***?" (Note: Some of the readers may know the phonetic acronym as "Whiskey Tango Foxtrot?")

Once we were back in Mike's vehicle, he floored it and kicked up gravel as we speed to sin city.

The moment caused us to laugh our asses off for the next 10 minutes.

Classic memories. I am so grateful to have known Mike and of course you too Jane.

I hope and pray your cherished memories will provide solace and courage to continue honoring Mike's memory.
God's speed and blessings.
Matthew Edmund Airey

Your Life's Takeaways:

Reflect on one or two experiences with someone who significantly stands out in a critical and very memorable moment you joyously remember and cherish? ____.

That someone could be currently in your life or passed on. List a memory that "stands the test of time." ____.

Tell me about a person (maybe a contemporary) whose good news or bad news shocked you and thoroughly forced you to reflect on current life, and maybe their lives. ____.

Chapter 9. My Best Friend's Wedding. "With Me, Free Me."

Choosing a life partner is one of the most difficult and intense circumstances. Why is that? The statistics are daunting, since approximately 50% of married couples make the wrong choice in one way or another and end in divorce. Choosing your marriage partner directly effects one's emotional and physical health and wealth. If the couples have children, they are responsible for the child's development and happiness. A family divorce can negatively impact a child's environment and their long-term wellbeing.

One of my best friends, Rob Maywood, encountered much trepidation contemplating his marriage decision. One evening, Rod said he had a dream that finally convinced him that his bride would be Emily. It was a beautiful story and a relief for my friend that he could proceed with confidence and love in his commitment to marriage.

I wrote the following poem the day after Rob shared his vivid dream. I am certainly, not a poet, but at times in my life, the words and phrases just come to me. Maybe this reflects some of your touching experiences and feelings.

For Rob and Emily
July 24, 2004

"With Me, Free Me"
One strange, peaceful night, God sent me a dream.
I've walked through the gauntlet of someones,
Each there for a purpose, there was a theme
I've searched in time for the quenching one.

With Me, Free Me
Come and make me whole
With Me, Free Me

Steadfast, but lonely, there to give
I've traveled, I've waited, and hoped too,
Joyous, a glimpse so close to live
I've let go times before, but now, it's so near.

With Me, Free Me
Take my hand and walk
With Me, Free Me

The dream I will believe in is you and me.
The past painful journey will be lighter with love.
All mind, body, and soul for us, as all will be.
Certain that together, with other's support, as one.

With Me, Free Me
Two as one, nothing to fear
With Me, Free Me

Your Life's Takeaways:

Describe the experience of writing a poem. ____.

Have you ever written a poem about your true emotions? ____.

Or after having a dream (or hearing about a dream, like the experience written above)? ____.

When was that? ____.

Where is that poem now? Can you recreate it? ____.

Can you compose a simple three-line poem to someone you love regarding your feelings? ____.

Can you write down those words to express that emotion now? ____.

If you are married, what marriage premises did you hope to build upon? ____.

Can write them down? ____.

If you are married, did your marriage build upon these premises? ____.

If they don't, constructively address them with your spouse.

Work together on these challenges and also continue the more joyous and productive aspects of your marriage and family.

Postscript: Rob and Emily's commitment to each other in faith and love encountered challenges. A few months after their wedding ceremony, Emily got seriously ill, but thankfully made a fully recovery.

And as the poem reads, "Two as one, nothing to fear. With Me, Free Me." together they walked passionately toward new family paths. This couple committed to adopting two children and sharing their treasures and talents selflessly with others it needs. They chose a dream to believe in and committed to it. Have you done the same?

Chapter 10: "From Far, Far Away"

Introduction: Frank (Farouk) N. Maywood, MD (June 30, 1931 – February 1, 2017) immigrated to the US (New York) in 1956 from Alexandria, Egypt as an Obstetrics and Gynecology Medical Doctor with $20 dollars in this pocket. He was the father of my dear friend, Robert M. Maywood, MD, and I met Frank in September 1980. He quickly became like a second father to me and was always giving toward me. I dearly loved Frank and would kiss him on his check, similar to my dad. I always admired Frank's work ethic that included early Saturday and Sunday early morning hospital rounds in a suit and tie and building and living the American Dream. His humor was infectious, but he endured life's losses and joys. Frank treated me like one of his sons since he was loving and challenging in a positive manner. He showed a genuine interest in my personal, education and work life and in my relationships. Frank's generosity toward me was overflowing as he paid for me to accompany the family on several trips and dinner celebrations. On one occasion, Frank had to take care of an emergency patient, and he needed someone he could trust to watch over his young daughter. I was honored Frank called me to help him.

I wrote the following poem about Frank's experiences, which began in Egypt near the beaches of Alexandria. Frank always loved the beach; as I did. Frank told me as a young boy, he would find shrapnel and artifacts from the World War II battles in Egypt. Frank's love of academics and medicine came from his father, who was a teacher. His mother died when Frank was child, but she instilled in him a sense of wonder, kindness, and close family values. The poem references Frank's far away journey from Egypt to America.

From Far, Far Away

From Far, Far Away I walk the shores of Kings and World War,
A youth with dreams of a new shore.
But first the study and work of a trade,
One of medicine and birth; one that I will persuade.

From Far, Far Away later I land on York Shore; so New,
With just an American Dream; money and riches so few.
The work, the grind, the time does not matter to me,
My best and love, is yet to be.

From Far, Far Away I draw close to love, a family of mine,
Love I encounter, and laughter many over time.
The pain of doubt and loss cuts deep in heart,
Far distance, yet close, at times sets me apart.

From Far, Far Away I live with a passion, love, and some wit,
Pray family and friends enjoy me, not forget.
Not medicine, nor life force me down today,
Since Loved Ones, I Still Feel you; From Not So Far, Far Away.

Frank, Goodbye and Thank You.
Matthew Airey. February 1, 2017.

Your Life's Takeaways:

Reflect on someone or maybe that someone is you, who has immigrated to the US and built and lived or is currently living the American Dream. ____?

What struggles (losses and joys) have they (or you) had to endure? ____.

Are there current struggles for you to overcome to experience the American Dream? ____.

Postscript: Frank's Memorial Service Program concluded with the following quote:

"Death opens a door out of a little, dark room into a great, real place where the true sun shines and we shall meet."

— C.S. Lewis, Till We Have Faces

Chapter 11: "Aunt Kathy, You're Not Singing Loud Enough!"

Introduction: Robert Christopher Engh (August 20, 1958 – January 2, 2006) was my first cousin, who had Down syndrome. In the late 1950's, it was still very common for the medical profession to recommended that Down syndrome infants be institutionalized. However, the sisters at the hospital correctly influenced my uncle and aunt to raise Robert in their home with their other five children. And they certainly did; Robert went to a specialized school, his family church, and eventually had a paying job.

Robert's dad, Uncle Don, was a World War II pilot and Los Angeles City Fire Captain. My Aunt Therese was my father's oldest sister. She was the first child, and my dad was the second child of nine Airey children). My oldest cousin and Godfather is Father Michael Engh, SJ. Robert was a kind soul, but he needed structure and caring guidance and his family helped to provide that discipline. Robert and I in the second group of Airey grandkids so we would naturally group together at family functions. Robert had a great sense of humor, and I remember one memory of him, and his large orange billed and white feathered duck. Robert's duck use to freely roam in his backyard, but during family outdoor celebrations, he would expect the duck to sit quietly next to the patio table. Robert knew this was an unreasonable expectation, but he humorously convenience his you cousins like me that this was possible. Robert would dramatically chase his pet around this yard. Robert's brother Greg commented, "Maybe that duck needs a new owner." "Maybe I need a new brother," was Robert's quick-witted response. Silly moments like that grew my fondness toward my cousin Robert.

The following few words are my reflections that I shared with Robert's family to emphasize the value of their affectionate dedication to Robert. I experienced it first-hand and revere the memories.

January 3, 2006

Uncle Don, Aunt Therese, cousins Mike, Steve, John, Kathleen, Gregory, and extended Engh family members:

Please accept our sincerest and heartfelt condolences from Christy, Garrett, Shane, Connor and I for the loss of your son and brother Robert. We have been praying for God's mercy for Robert and all of you for some time now.

Within our daily appeals I could not help but reflect on a few significant observations regarding Robert's meaningful life and the faithful family that supported him.

Witness.

When I was getting ready to make my confirmation, I remember our instructors telling us that we had to bear witness to Our Lord. As a teenager and a young man, I never really grasped the practical message of bearing witness.

However, the Engh Family was the very embodiment of bearing witness to Our Lord's commandment of love when it came to caring for their son and brother, Robert. Each family member seemed to take their individual turn throughout the years to reassure, guide, and comfort their son and brother. I cannot remember a time when there was ever a lack of patience and compassion when sharing their lives with Robert. I remembered then and now, how amazed I was and am, at the sheer magnitude of generosity that was put forth on a daily basis toward each other and especially toward Robert.

Something in Common.

Robert and I had something in common by being two of the only USC Trojan Fans in the bunch versus the Fighting Irish fans. I am grateful he shared his support and his victorious predictions with me. I am sure he is Fighting On with all of Saints right now. What a vision!

Comedy.

The joy Robert brought into so many lives is immeasurable. Here are a few of my fondest memories. I remember his uncles would sometimes affectionately kid around and tease Robert. When Robert was done with the conversation, he'd get that serious look and mischievous grin on his face and say something like, "Oh Joe or Oh Monk, no, no, I don't think so!"

On one occasion, we were singing Christmas Carols at the Engh's home, and Robert found it necessary to point out that his Aunt Kathy "wasn't signing loud enough!" A rage of infectious laughter ensued. Aunt Kathy was always a good sport. Great stuff.

May God Bless you all. Thanks, Matthew Airey

Your Life's Takeaways:

Reflect on one or two people who live with and embrace some type of mental or physical challenge. Who are they? ____.

What are their admirable qualities and behaviors? ____.

How do others around them react or observe this person (these people)? ____.

Have any of these individuals attended school with you? ____.

Or worked in the same setting with you? ____.

What experiences significantly stands out as a critical and very memorable moment that you joyously remember and cherish? ___.

How did they affect the lives of others? ___.

Chapter 12: "That's My Nephew, Matthew."

Introduction: Judith Audine Gerberick (February 15, 1939 – October 16, 2015) was my aunt (My Mother's Sister In law). The following few words are my reflective memories that I shared with Judy's family.

George, Audine, Amanda, Teresa, and Jim.

Each of your tireless efforts to support and heal Judy were remarkable and amazing to experience. You all came to her needs while she rested during her home care and visited her daily in the hospital. You encouraged her through her diabetes and infections, and you consoled her after she lost her leg due to poor circulation.

Please except my heartfelt and humble disclosure of some key memories of my Aunt Judy.

Judy always referred to me as Matthew. This was kind of special for me, since my classmates always called me Matt or Matty. But Judy was unfailing, and I remember this from an early age. I always felt a deep connection to her. It gave me a sense of belonging. This is hard for me to describe; it was just my sentiment. You can't see or touch it, but you know it is contained within you and others.

I remember Judy made me a sandwich one time when I was with you all at Doheny State Beach, California. I was sitting at the trailer table waiting, as Judy was in the kitchen. When she placed the sandwich in front of me, I quickly chomped it down. She smiled and laughed out loud. She remarked, "Matthew, the girls don't eat like that." Ha, good times.

After I graduated from college, I substituted for a while in the West Covina School District. There was one time I was substituting at Judy's school. I entered the classroom, and I saw her in the back of the classroom. But she didn't see me; so, I snuck up behind her and tapped her shoulder. Judy turned and said, "Oh my God honey, you scared me." Then, Judy gave me a big hug and kiss. The kids started to say, "Eeuh, Mrs. Gerberick." Judy said, "That's enough, this is my nephew, Matthew."

Judy truly loved the kid she taught. Her students had severe physical and learning challenges. But Judy relished in the quest to love and support them.

And the best for last, walnut balls. Walnut ball dough is comprised of butter, brown sugar, vanilla, sifted flour, salt, and finely chopped walnuts. After they are baked, the walnut balls are rolled and covered in powdered sugar. I would pop tons on these delicious treats into my mouth. Judy would always give me an extra holiday tin filled with them. I really appreciated all her special effort and time for me through the years making these treats. I do realize that there are other family baking talents since my cousin Audine now carries on that walnut ball tradition. Thanks for that.

Love you all. God's Speed. Matthew

Your Life's Takeaways:

Can you specifically think of an Aunt or an Uncle, who made you feel a sense of belonging (being part of them or their family group)? ___.

How did your Aunt or Uncle make you feel special? ___. Did they consistently say something or write something that was just between you and them? ___.

Have you told them or written to them to show your gratitude? ___. I am sure glad I did.

89

Postscript: Judy's Celebration of Life. November 5, 2015

Welcome to the Celebration of Life of Judith Audine Gerberick.

Thank you for all coming tonight and for supporting George, Terry, Jim, Audine, and Amanda.

We would all like to express our deep condolences on the loss of Judy.

My name is Matthew Airey.

I am George and Judy's nephew. My mother is George's sister, Marguerite.

I am Terry and Audine's cousin.

The family asked me to read some scripture and prayers.

These prayers are paraphrased from the Catholic Funeral Mass Ritual (Reference: United States Conference of Catholic Bishops).

Then, they will share their memories and heartfelt emotions with you.

God made us in His image, but we know we need His help.

We know we need each other at this time,

And we know we need His word and prayer.

Judy knew this too, and she prayed and received the sacraments in her life.

We are confident in God's mercy and love.

We are comforted that Judy is now truly in the presence of God.

<u>A reading from the second letter of Saint Paul to the Corinthians (4:13–5:1)</u>

We know that the one who raised the Lord Jesus will raise us also with Jesus,

and will bring us with you into his presence.

Yes, everything is for your sake,

so that grace, as it extends to more and more people,

may increase thanksgiving, to the glory of God.

So, we do not lose heart.

Even though our outer nature is wasting away,

our inner nature is being renewed day by day.

For this slight momentary affliction is preparing us

for an eternal weight of glory beyond all measure,

because we look not at what can be seen

but at what cannot be seen.

for what can be seen is temporary, but what cannot be seen is eternal.

For we know that if the earthly tent we live in is destroyed,

we have a building from God,

a house not made with hands, eternal in the heavens.

The Word of the Lord

A reading from the holy gospel according to John (11:32-45)

When Mary, the sister of Lazarus, came where Jesus was and saw him,

she knelt at his feet and said to him,

"Lord, if you had been here, my brother would not have died."

When Jesus saw her weeping, and the Jews who came with her also weeping,

He was greatly disturbed in spirit and deeply moved.

He said, "Where have you laid him?"

They said to him, "Lord, come and see."

Jesus began to weep.

So, the Jews said, "See how he loved him!"

But some of them said,

"Could not he who opened the eyes of the blind man

have kept this man from dying?"

Then Jesus, again greatly disturbed, came to the tomb.
It was a cave, and a stone was lying against it.
Jesus said, "Take away the stone."
Martha, the sister of the dead man, said to him,
"Lord, already there is a stench because he has been dead four days."
Jesus said to her,
"Did I not tell you that if you believed, you would see the glory of God?"
So, they took away the stone.
And Jesus looked upward and said,
"Father, I thank you for having heard me.
I knew that you always hear me,
but I have said this for the sake of the crowd standing here,
so that they may believe that you sent me."
When he had said this, he cried with a loud voice, "Lazarus, come out!"
The dead man came out, his hands and feet bound with strips of cloth,
and his face wrapped in a cloth.
Jesus said to them, "Unbind him, and let him go."
Many had seen what Jesus did, and believed in him.
The Gospel of the Lord.

A final prayer (Reference: United States Conference of Catholic Bishops)

Lord,
Judy is gone now from this earthly dwelling,
and has left behind those who mourn her absence.
Grant that we may hold her memory dear,
never bitter for what we have lost
nor in regret for the past,

but always in hope of the eternal Kingdom
where you will bring us together again.

May the love of God and the peace of the Lord
bless and console us
and gently wipe every tear from our eyes.
This we ask.
Amen.

Traditional Catholic Prayer to St Jude (Aunt Judy's Patron Saint).

Glorious St. Jude, with faith in your goodness, we ask your help today. As one of Christ's chosen Apostles, you remain a pillar and foundation of His Church on earth. You are counted, we know, among the elders who always stand before God's throne.

From your place of glory, we know you do not forget the needs and difficulties of Christ's little ones here, still struggling, like me, on the way home to God. Please intercede for us all, gracious St. Jude, and be with us in our daily toil and in all our necessities. In Christ's name, we appeal to you again today. Amen.

Chapter 13: "God Doesn't Have A Watch."

Introduction: The phrase "God doesn't have watch" is attributed to my supportive and kind neighbor, Michael "Big Mike" Byrd. Mike and I will share our life updates and tragedies with each other, and Mike consoled me with his phrase. His faithful delivery of the phrase and his concern for me was touching and profound (i.e. "It hit me like a ton of bricks.").

This phrase and its message served me well with a longtime friend. On Wednesday, April 23, 1975, I made my Catholic Confirmation. I have always liked dressing up in suits, since I was a little kid, and on this day, I was feeling pretty good about my attire. I wore a burgundy, blue and gray checked wide lapel sports coat, blue bell-bottomed cuffed slacks, and white and blue dress shoes (maybe with a slightly higher soft shoe heal too). Hey now, this was 1975.

After the ceremony, we gathered in the school playground, and my friend, Mike Frazzette, introduced me to his neighborhood friend, Donny Denison. "Holy Ned! I wish I could have longer hair, but that public school kid needs a haircut," I thought to myself. Mike mentioned that Donny was planning to play football with us when we go to Bishop Amat High School in the fall of 1976. "Ok cool. Nice to meet you Donny," as I shook his hand. "Matt, this is my sister Debbie."

Again, "Holy Ned!" Debbie was shy and so cute with her long blond hair. Remember I liked blonds. Debbie had gorgeous blue eyes. I smiled and shyly replied, "Hi, Debbie." In that moment little did I know that Donny and Debbie would remain my close friends during and after high school for over 45 years. On

Saturday, January 5, 1985, my mom, dad and I attended Debbie's wedding to Kirk Burns. Recently, while going through old boxes in the garage, and I found Debbie's date marked in my old 1985 calendar.

Here's the letter I wrote to Debbie after we saw each other and had a serious conversation before attending our high school football game on Friday, October 13, 2017.

Debbie. What you said to me about continuing your faith journey at the Bishop Amat High School Homecoming really had a deep impact on me. I have been thinking about this for some time now and praying about how I could best support you. Not force you; but support you in your faith journey.

I came up with two ideas. **One:** Enclosed is my rosary. I want you to have it. It is from Ireland; thus, the blessed green beads, shamrocks, and St. Patrick medal.

Keep it near you or in your purse or just hold it. The rosary servers as a prayer to Mary to interceded on our behalf while we reflect on Jesus' life and Mary's interaction within His life.

I've included some literature on how to pray the rosary, but do not get overwhelm by all of this. Just let it happen. Incredible blessings are possible.

I wanted to share a story (and you can share it with your family too), on one time in my life where praying the rosary and to Mary really helped me. And there have been many other times as well.

After our 9 and 0 undefeated Amat Freshman football season and after I played freshman basketball, I decided in the spring 1977 that I would start my own work-out program. I was happy with playing defensive end, but I knew I had a shot at starting at fullback my sophomore year; but I was not ready. I was big and pretty strong, but I didn't have the endurance or the mental toughness to play fullback.

I knew I had to change things up to improve. So, I started and ended each of my workouts kneeling and praying in front of the Amat Grotto (see Grotto Note Below) by myself. This really seemed to improve my confidence, ability, and the improvement I needed to play better. Note: The Amat Grotto is one of my favorite peaceful places on earth.

That season I started at fullback as I wanted, and your dad, Gary, really, really helped me. He would take me aside before or after practice or a game and coach me; he didn't want to embarrass me in front of my teammates. He was observant enough and cared enough to go out of his way for me. Your dad also wasn't afraid to kick my ass a few times, because he knew I could improve, even if I didn't know it then. I am eternally grateful to your dad, your mom, you and your brother for that type of kindness and caring. It made a big difference to me.

I hope that through some of your prayer devotion to Mary, our spiritual mother, that you will experience some of the same spiritual and life blessings that I have been so fortunate to experience. And I know through your husband, children, grandchildren, friends and family; you already have been enormously blessed.

Two: I searched Catholic Churches by your address, and I came up with the following.

When you're ready, and if you have a preference on one church over the other, I will help you research how to enroll in the Rite of Christian Initiation of Adults (RCIA). Depending on our schedules, I can even attend with you. Think about it. Pray about in. Remember, God doesn't have a watch, so you and He make up the timeline.

Debbie. Thanks for letting me contact you; and thanks for listening. Text or call me whenever.

Love ya. All the best. Matty

October 28, 2017

Conclusion: Nearly a year after I wrote this letter to Debbie, her mother, Jeanie, suddenly died of a heart condition at only 74 years old. Of course, Debbie and her entire family were crushed and saddened. I recalled then, my dad's early death, and the life changes that Debbie and her family were forced into emotionally. I reached out to Debbie and gently asked her to let me know when her mother's memorial service was.

The family decided to have a burial at sea service via a large vessel that travelled outside of Newport Beach, California harbor on Saturday, September 29, 2018. After we embarked, while heading out to sea, Debbie sat next to me. I felt her anxiousness and sadness, but I also sensed some calming relief within her.

"Matty, I brought the rosary you gave me," Debbie shared with me. I smile and hugged her. "I have decided to become a Catholic, and I want you to be my sponsor," Debbie said. "Wow, that's great. Of course, I will," I replied. I got misty eyed.

Talk about 'taking a pause.' Man, was I humbled that I had something (anything) to do with Debbie's faith development. Then, I thought about my immigrant great grandparents and my ancestors, who instilled and nurtured such an active faith. One that does not keep you "on the sidelines of life," but more so within the daily lives of others. We need to be 'in the game and in the trenches.'

Finally, after Debbie and I attended the required classes along with her husband, Kirk, and his sponsor, Melanie McIntrye, the April 20, 2019 Easter Vigil service conferred the sacraments of baptism, confirmation, and holy communion upon Debbie and Kirk. Additionally, the god their marriage blessed in the Catholic Church. But that was just the beginning of the story, this couple now encouraged their three daughters and their grandchildren to be baptized and join the church. I know they have a strong prayer life and consistently go to Mass and receive Holy Communion with their daughters, sons-in-laws and grandchildren. Wow, how amazing.

Your Life's Takeaways:

When have you currently taken the extra time to really listen to a family member or friend? ____.

Did you take a chance and offer encouragement? ____.

Did you speak up, rather than remaining on the sideline? ____.

I really appreciate when another close friend of mine, Dave Mitchell, will ask one of our friends, "What can we do to help?" When was the last time you offered to help? ____.

Be open to taking that risk, making yourself vulnerable, or putting some extra time for someone else. Your simple act of kind caring could have an enormous and lifelong impact on so many generations to come. List what you are going to do now to go out of your way for someone? ____.

Remember God Doesn't Have A Watch. Time is a relative human concept. You may find in your life that experiences or opportunities (i.e. a new job, a relationship) did not happened when you wanted them to (i.e. not on your time schedule, or your "watch"). My example is the time frame for my friend, Debbie's, Faith journey. I had no clue what was going to happen in those circumstance, but I did my best to reach out.

Share an experience in your life when the timing was not "yours," but things worked out well for you and / or others. ____.

Grotto Reference: In 1858, Saint Bernadette saw a vision of the Virgin Mary in a cave in Lourdes, France. A spring of water appeared, and countless miracles have occurred through immersion in it. Pilgrims eventually built a large church near the grotto and it quickly attracted thousands of people from around the world. The reputation of the Lourdes Grotto in France spread like wildfire and imitation grottoes were quickly built to honor Mary. They are man-made rock formations with a Statute of the Blessed Virgin Mary.

Chapter 14: "Who has the X on their forehead?" Business Reflections.

Introduction: I have over 30 years of business and consulting experience. Through that time, I gathered assembled 18 reflective and impactful quotes from managers and family members that have shaped my strategic and tactical leadership and personal style. I invite you to read and reflect on these sayings and relate them to your current business and personal character and document your notes.

Business Reflection 1:
"Who has the X on their forehead?" Jack Harris.

Jack Harris was a tough and direct manger, but a supportive and consulting one. His "threatening but effective question" was intended to determine accountability and organizational protocol. Re-phrasing, "who is doing what when?' and "who in the organization is responsible for managing results?" This quote "Who has the X on their forehead?" is a reference to 'X marks the target I am aiming for' or 'X marks the spot on a treasure map.' This quote gives clarity and direction of what tasks are to be completed. Jack forced and challenged my colleagues and me to have a clear understanding of our role. We needed to understand the organizational protocols that needed to be followed to fulfill project and transaction objectives within hierarchical and matrixed reporting structures. Who has the need to know? There may be a direct linear reporting organization, which dictate who receives status and data. Within a matrix organization, there may be peripheral or 'dotted lined' reporting structure that requires status and data to be shared with other stakeholders or influencers. Your organizational customers should help you answer the question 'Who has the need to know what and when?'

As a professional courtesy, who else should review be aware of status of data? Defining these accountability tasks and communication plans supports a "no surprises" (or at lease limiting them) approach. As a side note, professional courtesy includes giving responsible or impacted parties the "heads-up" consideration with the goal of fostering collaboration and strategic alignment. Jack would suggest to me and tell me, "Matt, Go walk over to finance and give them a draft copy of your report with my handwritten note attached."

Your Life's Takeaways:

Do you know what you are accountable for within your business organization (aka "the X on your forehead" means you will deliver what? And when?)? List them. ____.

What are you accountable for within your family and friendships? ____.

How can you help your team members and family members to better understand what you are accountable for and what they are accountable for? ____.

Business Reflection 2:
"It's a process, not an event." Jack Harris.

My impatience and lack of experience was usually put back into a more realistic and manageable business and technical process focus, as Jack repeated this quote to me. The quote was a nicer way to encourage my planning, measurement, and persistence processes within daily operations and project management. In other words, your work (Matt) is not done in one hour or a day, it takes time and some patience. The quote applies to one's business and personal life.

Your Life's Takeaways:

How can you improve your business and technical leadership skills and results by exercising more tactical planning and pragmatic patience? ___.

Are your business time lines and goals reasonable and based on real facts and processes? ___.

What current event in your Personal Life should represent more of a current process? ___.

What are you most impatient about in your Life? ___.

Is the event something you can really influence, or should your approach be more of a process? ___.

Business Reflection 3:
"Matt, you're a pain in the ass." Jack Harris.

Again, Jack's style and delivery was unconventional and was certainly different from my MBA training and the large corporation traditions I had experienced. He balanced candor with rewarding work performance. Especially since in my younger days I could have practiced more humility and silence. Thankfully, I quickly learned not to say the first thing that comes to my mind, and more appropriately respond to Jack's first "off the record" performance appraisal of me versus being ungrateful and disingenuous. I love retelling this story.

"Matt, you're a pain in the ass, but you did a lot of good work. Here's your money." Jack succinctly stated as he handed me a piece of paper with summarizing my work performance bonus, stock, and stock options.

Jack paused as I hastily reviewed the document contents.

"Any questions?" Jack impetuously queried.

"No sir. Thank you." I responded correctly, thankfully.

The document relieved that Jack had managed to reward my performance with the additional compensation of a bonus, stock, and stock options that were valued at approximately 50% of my salary. I was speechless, which at many times is a good thing. I never estimated that this remuneration was in the realm of positivity. Thanks Jack. Rest in Peace.

Your Life's Takeaways:

When have you had a business experience with a manager, who went out of their way to reward you, recognize your fine performance, or support your career advancement? ____.

As a Business Leader, is there a current opportunity where you should go out of your way of a team member? ____.

Should stand up a team member's sound reputation?

Within your current Personal Relationships, is there a circumstance that demands your commitment of engagement and display of gratitude whether as the "giver or receiver"? ____.

Business Reflection 4:
"Does anybody get off their f*ing lazy asses and talk to anyone anymore?" Dick Byrne**

Introduction: I was working at a small consulting firm in 1998 where Dick Byrne was our Chief Operations Officer. Dick was engaged, enthusiastic, and strategic. I reported my statuses to him frequently, and we organized my team's work queues and focused on performance metrics. Dick challenged and actively supported me. He was sarcastic and humorous but caring of others.

This was the dawn of the internet and email. Email began to take on a daily cadence of basic communication, replacing many meetings and many phone calls. Emails have the benefit of "documenting, what I call an audit trail." Particularly with younger people at the time (and even within today's age), younger team members grabbed onto this new technology; and they integrated emails into 24 x 7 communications.

However, there are some extreme limitations to emails. There are many business situations where emails are the total substitute for basic team member conversations and at times productive confrontation and problem solving. In my example, my co-workers would email back and forth when they sat less than 10 feet away from one another (i.e. one cube away). There would be exchange of tens of tens of emails on simple communications without any resolution. One such "ineffective email trail," was emotionally escalated (aka the email was forwarded to) to the leader, inspiring the above quote. Yes, the language usage was profane, but I thought was also profound and prophetic. Although the quote included some very "technical language (aka "Not the King's English"), the statement really stressed an integral and foundational business and technical operations approach. I found that I quickly incorporated the approach into my leadership style and my strategic daily management.

The underlining approach our leader in operations and finance was attempting to encourage was that after two or three unresolved emails, you may need to (or should definitely) get up out of your chair and go talk your team member. Listen to other people. Set up a meeting with an agenda to start to focus on strategy tactics, a plan, and a resolution. Solve the problem and move forward. I still find after over 30 years in business, and 20+ years of using email and the Internet, avoidant communication is still very pervasive in the workplace. My rule of thumb is if two or three emails does not resolve an issue or specifically delegated and document roles and responsibilities, then you have got to take collaborative action.

Be the better leader. Be the better person. Be the one that's proactive and walk a few feet maybe a few hundred feet to reach out to your clients and your colleagues. I am encouraging my younger readers to appreciate, and, at times, practice this approach. Additionally, make it a daily practice to walk around and say hello to your team members and customers. Now, I'm not debating the efficiency of emails and technology including groupware, video conferencing and instant messaging. I'm not debating the efficiency of having an audit trail to protect what was said what was agreed to (that is my current practice). However, there is no substitute for personal and professional rapport, trust, and credibility that should be built among colleagues and customers over time. Again, the prophetic question remains today. Doesn't anybody get up and go talk to people anymore?

<u>Your Life's Takeaways:</u>

Consider evaluating your current email, texts and instant messaging) tactics and style. Make sure that you use concise and positive content to help resolutions and results prevail. Never include offensive, accusatory or non-productive personal content in emails. In many cases, emails are "legally discoverable" for corporations or individuals. Do your emails reflect what you would want managers, friends and family members to read? List opportunities for you to improve or change your email tactics and style? ____.

Supplementary, the current consistent use of cell phones and laptops in meetings is counterproductive. I strongly advise against their use in meetings, unless there is a critical system of safety incident being managed or avoided. Observe the most engaged and effective team members in meetings. I estimate that most of them proactively listen, maintain eye contact, and write down their notes versus being distracted with their cell phones or laptops. What are your experiences with similar circumstances? ____.

What do you need to currently change within your communication and engagement behaviors to become a better person or leader? ____.

Business Reflection 5:
"When in doubt, drive for results." Dick Byrne

Your Life's Takeaways:

Within your business environment, what "noise or misinformation" is limiting the pursuit of "driving for results?" ____.

What "doubts" (negative attitude, gossip, selfish behaviors, potential ethical issues, and unsuccessful initiatives) should you currently avoid aligning focus on your organization's results? ____.

As a leader, what can you do to better define and align the "desired results" of the company? ____.

In your current personal life, what do you need to do to "drive for results?" ____.

Business Reflection 6:
"It's not what you make, it's what you keep." Alan Dunn

Your Life's Takeaways:

Does your organization properly control expenses?? Is there too much focus on just revenues? ____.

What strategies and tactics does your organization use to manage revenue and expenses? ____.

Within your current personal finances, what expenses (cash outflows) do you need to better control and balance to keep (save and invest) more money? ____.

Do you have a documented budget that is reviewed every three months? A three-month (or fiscal quarter) review period is a proactive approach to analyze trends, budget and expense changes, and budget variances. ____.

Within your current Personal Finances, how can you increase or improve your income (salary, investments, business revenue)? ___.

What is your income forecast over the next two years? ___.

Matt's Most Personal Business Reflections:

Business Reflection 7:
"You don't get rich on salary." My dad, Edmund Francis Airey, Jr.

My dear father was an educator and a tireless volunteer, not a businessperson or investor. However, this simple charter captured the necessity for long term investments to produce more wealth than a paycheck. I am humbly grateful for my dad's and mom's generosity.

Your Life's Takeaways:

What non-salary actions do you need to currently invest in to increase your wealth? List short term and long-term actionable strategies. ___.

Business Reflection 8:
"If our world is only limited to the earth we stand on, it's really not worth living."
My dad, Edmund Francis Airey, Jr.

Again, my dad's faith in the eternal afterlife is reflected in his quote. However, he did not ridicule another's riches. Dad was just suggesting a type of "Spiritual Detachment toward worldly possessions." My dad was just as excited and proud with buying a new car as a next-door neighbor. But he realized, "You can't take it with you when you die, and it did not necessarily help anyone get to heaven."

Your Life's Takeaways:

Is there something (i.e. an earthly possession) that you are obsessed with securing or continue to own? ____.

How has your focused obsession limited you from currently making your life worth living for you? ____. Making your life worth living for others? ____.

Name a person who has many possessions but appears down to earth and genuinely concerned for the wellbeing of others and themselves (and their eternal life)? ____.

Business Reflection 9:
"Buy land, they're not making it anymore." Mark Twain.
Repeated continuously by my grandfather, Papa Ed (Edmund Francis Airey, Sr.)

Maybe in my next manuscript, I will write and share more insights of my family ancestors and values. My grandfather was a sailor in the Merchant Marines, who then became a tugboat captain in San Pedro, California. After a few years of marriage and his first of nine children (dad was number two), Papa was given an opportunity to become a rancher when his father-in-law gave my grandmother and him a large portion of land to farm during America's Great Depression. Through savings and various land sales, Papa purchase and exchanged properties as a long-term investment. Historically speaking, land appreciates over years and decades versus daily stock fluctuations. My grandfather used time and years and years of holding and owning property as an investment strategy. My grandfather considered time as "his land investment partner." "God Bless All of My Great – Great Grandparents, Great Grandparents and Grandparents."

Your Life's Takeaways:

What land investments do you currently hold? ____.

What land investments / purchases should you / could you target for investment as part of your diversified savings portfolio within your risk tolerance? High (aggressive risk and higher potential gain or loss). Medium (moderate risk and moderate potential gain or loss), or Low (lower risk and lower potential gain or loss)? ____.

Have you considered? Should you consider becoming an investor / owner in a land or commercial property partnership? ____.

Or is becoming or remaining a sole landowner more supportive of your risk tolerance and investment strategy? ____.

Research whether REITs (Real estate investment trust) stocks or ETFs (exchange-traded fund) make sense within your land investment strategy. List your decision. ____.

Business Reflection 10:
"Do the hardest job first." Papa Ed.

Papa's adage took me some time to adjust to and to maintain, while I was working on the Airey Ranch with him." There were two aspects of this strategy that took me years to appreciate (Yes, sometimes I am a slow learner. Ha).

First, you're fresher and have more energy and focus at the beginning or your workday versus the middle or end of your day. This reflects hard physical ranch work or critical thinking skills.

Second, one experiences an internal sense of one's self-esteem of accomplishing difficult tasks, then, moving through the less strenuous and tedious tasks." Again, for me it took me years to put into practice, I try my best to dive into my most difficult tasks first, after I plan my approach and establish reasonable milestones.

Your Life's Takeaways:

What current hardest job have you been putting off in the place of easier tasks? ____.

What is the hardest job that you can make more productive or can improve? ____.

Your personal life? ____. In a relationship?

List the hardest Jobs you need to do first regarding your Mind, Body, and Soul? ____.

Business Reflection 11.01:
"Don't spend my money for me." Papa Ed.

One day, Papa was having me help him work on his 1941 Ford Tractor. It seemed to me that we would fix one tractor problem, and another would pop up. So, I whimsically questioned, "Papa, why don't you just buy a new tractor?" Holy Ned! The thunder of the heavens rained down on me. "Don't spend my money for me." Papa ordered me, much like a ship captain. How presumptuous and disrespectful my teenage problem-solving skills were?

Man, was I put in my place. Not another word was spoken between us that day, other than a request for tools or what my next job was. It seemed instantaneously, I ameliorated my appreciation for respecting money and spending, and more so, the spending of other's money from that quote (experience). Reflecting, Papa was not only making his point with me but was challenging me; and he had confidence in me that I could take it. I currently attempt to be more sensitive to the intricacies regarding professional or personal budgets and financial investments, while "valuing it as my money."

As a final example of Papa's more tempered approach, consider his following statement to me.

Business Reflection 11.02:
"If you don't have patience to teach, you're not worth much."
Papa Ed.

This was Papa's encouragement after I apologized to him for stalling the ranch truck on an inclined road three times in a row. He just looked straight ahead and commented. I then relaxed, restarted the vehicle, and shifted ahead in low gear.

Your Life's Takeaways:

How can you have a more balanced appreciation and respect for money and spending, and more so, the spending of other's (professional and personal) money? ____.

When have you demonstrated patience in teaching someone a new skill? ____.

What current opportunities are available for you to practice more patience within your work or home environments? ____.

Business Reflection 12:
"Do you trust them?" Retired United States Marine Corps Colonel Ken Brown, 1998.

Ken was a Technology Director who I worked with. He had distinguished military and technology training and career experience, and Ken took a keen interest in my professional and personal development. One day, I confidentially told Ken that was thinking about leaving our present firm and take on new position with a different company. Ken intently listened my descriptions. I could sense his disappointment in me leaving and his appreciation for the enormous opportunity presented to me.

Ken paused and took a breath and asked just one question of me, "Do you trust them?" I respectfully paused and contemplated Ken's question and my answer. I mentally tried to ascertain what criteria Ken would consider a reasonable and concise answer.

Immediately, I reflected on his high standards of integrity and technical work quality. My answer, "Yes, because this new position is a direct referral from a professional and personal friend, who I have successfully worked with in the past." Ken sensed my serious contemplation and reasoning and replied, "Matt. Congratulations. I will miss you. Best of luck to you. I know you will do well. Let me know if you need anything." (Ken. Thank you for all of your support through the years. Thank you for your service to our nation.)

Your Life's Takeaways:

What organizations, people and circumstances do you currently mistrust? ____. Do examples include broken promises or guidelines and inconsistent management practices? ____.

Why? ____. Is there a realistic and practical path to fortifying that trust? ____.

What can you do, or should you do to promote more trust? ____.

If a true sense of trust cannot be established, what is steps do you need to take to transition to a trust-based affiliation? ____.

Business Reflection 13:
"Don't assume that people will come to the same conclusions as you. Tell them what your conclusions are." Matthew Airey.

This is my adage to alleviate doubt and promote clarity in professional and personal experiences. I try not to be too demonstrative or pontifical when following my motto, but at least I concisely state my suggestions with the intention of sharing my viewpoint. I have found my approach tends to more accurately list business alternatives to consider. Then, the management will determine the alternative to follow or I will efficiently provide direction to my supervised resources. This tactic allows for more accountability and a method of managing desired conclusions. A helpful leader will clearly answer resource questions regarding the provided directions.

Your Life's Takeaways:

What current conclusions have you accurately articulated to your work team members and your family and friends? ____.

What methods can you implement to better share your conclusions? ____.

What do you need to currently change about your style to get your point of view across? ____.

Business Reflection 14:
"Surround yourself with people smarter than you." IBM training 1998.

The value of this guideline is that most likely we do not always possess all the answers or creative problem-solving aptitude. Thus, a combination of your capabilities and capacities when collaborated and aligned with others produces a more effective and desired results. We can usually learn something new and improve our skills as a result of working with intelligent and sharp team members. In this "dog eats dog world," this work approach to team building and professional association is counter intuitive. It is natural to feel threatened and uneasy with very intelligent resources on your team or reporting to you. However, work through your uneasy feeling and more forward toward continuous improvement.

Your Life's Takeaways:

When have you currently avoided hiring or surrounding yourself with people, who are smarter than you? ____.

What improved results occurred when you joined forces with people, who have an advanced knowledge based? ____.

Business Reflection 15:
"Focus. Do your job. Have fun."
Matt Airey's advice to his sons, while participating in your sports and school activities.

While trying to encourage my sons to do their best and enjoy their participation development, we came up with this simple motto. We know that children can be over coached and unwarranted pressure can be thrusted upon them. Focus seemed to be foundational in increasing performance (succeed at your job) and enjoyment (having fun). This motto is applicable to our adult opportunities and challenges.

Your Life's Takeaways:

Do you currently need to apply more "focus" in "doing" your professional and personal "jobs?" ____.

What are some initial and meaningful approaches in increasing your focus and performance? ____.

Our professional work environments cannot always be frivolous (aka fun). But what actions can you and your team members pursue to increase your work satisfaction and self-worth during your workday? ____.

We spend so much of our adult lives working that a sense of one's fulfillment should be a benefit of a healthy and productive career. Do you need to strategize a career move versus wasting more time in a negative and adverse work environment? ____.

Business Reflection 16:
"If it's meant to be, it will be." J.M. Barrie.
Imparted to Matt Airey by a close friend, Devin Hornick.

Devin put me at an immediate relaxed state when he shared this quote with me, while I was very anxious about being offered a new job. The intent of the quote is not to take things so dramatically or seriously as long as you prepared and performed your best.

When I quickly researched some background on this quote, I found the following on www.quora.com: "What it directly translates to is "if (that relationship) is meant to be (a lasting relationship), it will (end up that way, no matter what the path is that leads there)." It implies a faith that things that are meant to happen **will** happen, so that you don't have to try to force something or worry about it."

My dad repeated Saint Augustine's quote to me, "Pray as though everything depended on God. Work as though everything depended on you."

Your Life's Takeaways:

When have you currently been overly anxious about an event or a relationship? ___.

How can you increase your confident contentment that you did your best and whatever happens, happens? ____.

Have you ever had a relationship or an event just "fall into place" as you became more positive and peaceful with your approach and the outcome? ___.

Introduction: Monsignor Cremins, Father John, was the Chaplain at Bishop Amat Memorial High School. Father John prominently led music classes throughout the Los Angeles Archdiocese for decades and taught my dad in the college seminary. Father John worked with and cared for my "Aunt Wiggy" (Sister Margaret "Peggy" Airey, who died of terminal breast cancer in 1974).

When I started my freshman year of high school, my dad told me, "Make sure you say hello to Father John for us. He's one of the good ones." My dad's direction provided an endearing and influential friendship with Father John that resulted in a lifetime, deep-seated moral compass and positive attitude for my life. He influenced me to be very aware of the people around me and their emotional temperaments, and I suspect my future writing efforts will have to spend more emotional effort to describe the gravities of Father John's legacy and Christ-like compassion.

Business Reflection 17:

"Your generosity will come back tenfold." Monsignor John Patrick Creminis.

This quote appears in this Business Reflections Chapter, because Father John said it to me in the context of my participation in the business work environment. Here's what he meant. Your generosity means your work dedication and ethic. It means your genuine non –political investment in others' success and development and delivery of the highest quality delivery of services and products to your customers.

"Will come back to you tenfold" means your personal and organization's financial reward will richly profit from your generous perseverance. The quote does not literally mean 10 X (i.e. ten times the profits or ten times your annual bonus amount). The sentiment is a reminder that your work can make good things happen, and usually the best growth results and longevity are brought about by a company's superior customer delivery and operations. Customers generally become repeat buys if they have a positive customer experience. Superior operations usually translate into higher efficiencies and profits. However, it also refers to the additional benefits of intellectual, emotional, and spiritual progress with individuals and organizations due to their outward focus.

Conclusion: This quote and years of reflections and experiences led me to share one of my leadership maxims:

Business Reflection 18:
"Things just don't happen; people make them happen."
Matthew Airey.

Your Life's Takeaways:

Share a work experience when "your generosity" resulted in positive results for you, your team, and your organization. ____.

What is a current work example where "generosity" (yours or others) has been limited and caused limited success? ____.

What could you do to increase the amount of "generosity?" ____.

List some manners in which you can genuinely invest in others' success and development and deliver the highest quality delivery of services and products to your customers. ____.

Chapter 15: "Nana, Where's My Microphone?"

Introduction: I recently found several spiral notebook lined papers stapled together in the left- hand top corner with my mother's hand printed copy of my 1984 USC college course writing project. This was a story I had written out in long hand for my journalism class. Since I had terrible cursive skills, my mom would offer to clearly write out the story so I could type out the content later. What a treasure to find and re-appreciate the story's content and personal reflections. It reminded me of the quote by Mark Twain: "Write what you know." I tried to do that. Please do not think that the story's sentiments reflect my belief that I have exception talents. I simply cherish my fond recollections as a man, who is growing older and increasingly sentimental and thankfully a little more inhibited than in my youth.

"Nana, where's my microphone?" I used to ask my grandmother (Josephine Termine Gerberick, February 1, 1911 – June 9, 1972). When I was about age three, nana would sometimes take care of me on Saturdays. Nana's response to this common question would always be the same. She would take her Fuller Brush white, plastic strainer and tie a piece of string to the end of it. This, of course was my microphone. Next, she had to supply me with some musical accompaniment, while I took my homemade microphone into her living room (Rosemead, California). Nana would put on my Roger Miller "King of the Road" 1965 album on the Hi-Fi. It was the perfect way to keep me busy, because I would literally pass the day away singing for hours. Unfortunately, I did not have to interrupt Nana's housework when she had to change the record for me. But then again, doesn't every struggling young performer need a little family support?

Actually, from all the stories my family tells, I get the impression that I have been enjoying music ever since my birth. It seems almost as if I sang and danced before I could talk and walk. Although music was never forced upon me, luckily it was easily accessible. My mother recalls I would seek out music to listen to on transistor radios and dance programs to watch on television on my own. At this early stage no one actually instructed me in singing and dancing. Instead I took my cues from the voices I heard and the singers I watched.

When I used to watch "American Bandstand," I would pull out my dresser drawer and turn it over on the floor. This naturally was my stage, and I would stand on it with my miniature plastic guitar. I guess I was trying to re-create all the props, procedures, and performances I had seen on the show. My grandfather (Papa Jim, James Henry Gerberick, 1908 – 1989) also recalls a trip we took up to his mountain cabin (Big Bear Lake, California). Apparently, I supplied the entertainment for the ride. While sitting between him and Nana in his new 1966 blue and white Ford Pickup, I bounced up and down on the seat and spontaneously blurted out self-composed song lyrics. Papa said they got a great laugh out of my energetic, uninhibited behavior.

It may appear that my reactions are the same as many others, but I know that the energy I feel is unique unto myself. I believe the reason why I like music so much is because of this energetic element. Music has an energy force that can drive me to dance or compel me to feel romantic. The emotions I have concerning the music I like are difficult to explain.

For instance, if I am driving along and suddenly hear a song I really like, I probably show a common response. Since I am able to play the drums (I used to play the drums), I usually start drumming on something. I pound out rhythms on my dashboard or on my knees. Then, as I have done since my childhood, I sing along. In doing so, I attempt to capture the emotions communicated through the music and lyrics. For example, when I hear

"My Generation" by The Who I imitate the proud anger surrounding the song. However, my emotions are probably distinct from those intended by the songwriters or those felt by most fans. I do not concentrate on the songs' youthful statement. Instead my feelings reflect a specific reference point in my life experience: the excitement and pleasure I personally encountered when I saw The Who perform at the Los Angeles Memorial Coliseum on Friday, October 29, 1982 (The Clash / T-Bone Burnett. The frame of reference I have for experience a song always influences my reaction to it. Relating music to my personal experience says is the central reason behind the enjoyment I received from music.

When I think about the music I prefer most, it appears that my opinions revolve around the musical performer. It was when I take a liking to the individual performer that I received more pleasure from the music. For example, one of my favorite musical entertainers is Elvis Presley.

As a child I watched his old movies on television and was familiar with some of his songs, but I only began to admire him later on in my life. My early exposure to Elvis does not serve as my frame of reference for enjoying his music. However, when I was 17 years old, my friend Jason Wilson and I saw "This Is Elvis" at the Avco Theater in Westwood. This is the experience my emotions reflect whenever I hear Elvis singing.

When reviewing that movie, I inevitably discovered many beautiful and not so appealing characteristics of Elvis' personality. Yet, I do not wish to comment on Elvis' or any other performer's personal lifestyles. Although the private side of the performer is often interesting to learn about, I discovered that night that I am mainly concerned about a performer's music and stage presence. I discovered that Elvis projected the energy that I search for in music. His music can make me feel sorrowful as well was enthusiastic.

For crowd upon crowd of screaming young women, one of Elvis's most in my are energetic qualities was, of course, his rapid hip-shaking movements. However, I also felt his charismatic qualities when I watched him perform ballads. For his many fans, Elvis' jerking motions made him pleasurable to watch, and his voice fluctuations made him satisfying to hear. Elvis is the epitome of rock 'n' roll. Personally, I see his power and influence as attributable to the vitality of his musical expression.

Another personal Elvis reflection occurred on the day of his death, Tuesday, August 16, 1977. In the early afternoon after my high school football practice, I stepped off the Los Angeles Rapid Transit District Bus #482 and strolled up the sidewalk toward my home. I noticed that my dad's friend, John Reynolds, had his Harley parked in front. As I walked through the door and walked in the kitchen, I saw my dad and John. "Hey Matt. Did you hear Elvis died?" John reported. I tilted my head in disbelief and looked at my dad. "Yeah, we just heard it on the news." Dad replied. "That's terrible," I lamented. "Elvis was only 42 years old." John and Dad didn't say anything after that, since they knew I was a big fan.

One of my favorite musical groups is The Rolling Stones. Although I have had many reference points regarding my liking of the Rolling Stones, my first experience refers to a time about five years ago. I was napping at my friend Donny Denison's house before we both had to go to evening football practice on Wednesday night. Suddenly Mick Jagger's voice began to echo in my ears. Donny was using the song "Shattered" as my wake-up call. After the song's first verse, I quickly jumped up and began to chant as if I possessed Mick's noticeable lips. My lip movements were accompanied by an imitation of Mick's chicken strut dance move. Donny reinforced my efforts by telling me that I had done a pretty good imitation. That moment of acceptance was the beginning of my future attempts at Jagger imitations.

As a USC freshman, one of my favorite songs of the gang on the second floor of Birnkrant Residence Hall was "She's So Cold." The popularity of this song gave me the opportunity to further develop my sound and moves. During the dorm beer parties, I used Charlie Smith's hairbrush as my microphone. C'mon it was clean. Charlie was a neat freak. Naturally, I had outgrown my white plastic Fuller Brush strainer.) I carefully held the hairbrush to capture a more refined Jagger look. My dorm buddies praise my imitation and always added to the festivities with their backup vocals.

In the Rolling Stones, and especially Mick Jagger's performance, I easily find that element of energy that I favor in performances. Mick's high-stepping and hip swaying dance techniques always communicate excitement to his audience. Keith Richards's guitar strumming shoulder movements characterize an almost rhythm and blues feeling. ("You got to shock them, show them.") Moreover, I find some of the Stones music to be energetic and thought-provoking. For example, I find personal meaning in the verse, "You can't always get what you want ... you get what you need." I sometimes desire more luxuries, but then I realize that I do already have the necessities of life.

Of course, the emotions I feel when I hear the Stones have been enhanced by another major reference point: their Friday, October 9, 1981 performance at the Los Angeles Memorial Coliseum. I will remember the details of the anticipation before the concert and the performance itself for many years. KLOS 95.5 FM announced that the Stones' tickets were going on sale at 10 AM on September 9 at the Los Angeles Sports Arena. I was so startled by the 9 a.m. news that I nearly tripped over my Levi's when trying to step into them. I knew right away that I had to get tickets without any delay. I telephone my friend Rob Maywood to tell him about the radio announcement of the ticket sales. First of all, Rob had to go to the Ready Teller automated teller machine, because we had to have cash to purchase the tickets. We decided that I would ride my bike over to pick him up at

Security Bank in about 15 minutes. When I met Rob, he jumped on the handlebars of my black cruiser, and we started off for the sports arena. I eagerly pump the pedals, enthusiastically repeating, "We're going to see The Stones! We're going to see The Stones!" As we traveled south on Figueroa Street, it became apparent this was a reality: within a month I would experience my favorite rock 'n' roll band live on stage.

The ticket line was relatively short, and we quickly positioned ourselves. A long time, diehard Stones' fan with long hair and a worn leather jacket was in front of us. As we talked, he mentioned that each person could only purchase eight tickets. We were certain that we had at least 14 other friends, who wanted to attend this concert. Rob determined that another Ready Teller ATM visit was required. Once he returned with an additional $120, we were set. We purchased 16 tickets. However, I could not get any "satisfaction" from purchasing just 16 tickets; this was just too great of an opportunity. I was certain that we had more friends who yearned to experience The Stones. Once again, Rob set off on a quest for additional cash, while I waited in line. Upon his return, I again approached the ticket window on stated, "I would like eight tickets to see The Rolling Stones please." By 11 AM I was sitting in Rob's dorm room drinking a Stroh's beer from Detroit and handling a total of 24 concert tickets.

At the time my favorite song will "Start Me Up." This tune became my anthem, because everybody knew how much I liked The Stones, and how excited I was about the concert. Finally, the greatly anticipated day arrived. I began my day early with coffee and an egg and toast breakfast followed by hot shower. I got dressed and walked from my apartment on Portland Street to the Birnkrant dorm where I linked up with the most of our party of 24. As our small group walked toward the Coliseum, I was amazed to see a huge crowd gathering. It was only 10 AM, but we had to search for relatively short entrance line. After an hour's wait in line, I concluded that this day was going to be very exhausting. Upon our entrance into the stadium, we raced towards the field and made our claim to a spot. From then on, I grew increasingly impatient, because I knew I would have to combat this large crowd during a lengthy wait.

The huge orange, pink, and blue curtains were finally opened at 6:30 p.m. after three warm-up bands (Prince, George Thorogood and The Destroyers, The J. Geils Band), a hot dog, a Coke and plenty grass stains I figured I'd earn the right to see The Stones perform. I noticed a figure racing behind the curtains, and I exclaimed, "There he is!" The public address system projected the announcement: Ladies and Gentlemen the Rolling Stones! Within 15 feet of my eyes stood the creators of the music I enjoy the most. "Yaa!" I yelled. The smile I wore summarize my warm and happy feeling. Mick and the boys were everything in person that they were on film. Even Ronnie Wood and Keith Richards jogged around the extended stage. Their instrumental performance was tight and together. Charlie Watts's drumming was graceful, and he had his usual grin. Bill Wyman played his base without moving from his fixed stage position or breaking a smile. After 2 1/2 hours, 90,000 fans certainly had experienced a musical happening. I was part of that experience, and that day serves as a point when my musical motions reached a peak.

Seeing a live performance can add so much to my appreciation of artist. I remember being a little skeptical about Rod "The Mod" Stewart, while many of my high school friends thought he was great. It wasn't until I watched him from my Universal Amphitheater 22nd row seat a few years later that I was convinced that his athletic show displayed all the energy I looked for in a performer - from his mid-air twirls to his very passionate voice. Since I like to focus on voice quality and characteristics movements, I then developed my Rod Stewart imitation. This soon earned me a new nickname. On my cake for my 20th birthday, my friends had written "Happy Birthday, Matt the Mod."

Like many others, my first musical training was in the church choir. During fifth grade at St. Martha's grade school in La Puente, California, my class had the opportunity to volunteer for the church choir. About five girls and five boys, including myself, followed Sister Teresita to the church. Sister was a tall woman, standing about 5'10". She had a strong frame that I thought accounted for her immense vocal capacity, as well as her ability to frighten children into behaving. My classmates and the other volunteers from the upper grades crowded around the church organ in the choir loft as she played. After a week of practice, she decided to tape record us so she could evaluate our progress. I felt the tape recording was very important, and I was prepared to perform at my highest level as sister motion for us to begin the song, I joyfully blurted out the first word. Sister Teresita stopped after the first verse and rewound the tape. The recording was accented by a "Pah sound" I shouted for the song's opening word" "Praise." My friend, Jeff Parriott, nudged my shoulder as sister grinned at me and said, "Let's try that again." I lowered my head and laughed. However, I realized that my singing had to be controlled. Although I had done so in childhood, I could no longer sing what and how I pleased.

My musical training advanced when I began to take private drum lessons in the seventh grade. On Saturdays my father would drive me down West Holt Street in Pomona to the Universal Drum Center. For three years I took lessons from Doug Brucher, whom I remember as a kind man. He was about 28 years old when I began my lessons. Doug had a tall and thin frame, big smile, and he wore thick glasses. He graduated from college and worked at General Dynamics for four years. However, he became bored with the field of engineering and resumed his career in drumming.

Doug seemed very happy about his decision to quit his job. He practiced long and hard to refine his craft. Doug's enthusiasm influenced me to care about practicing my drums. The best thing I liked about Doug was that he was very patient with me. Without ever foot forcing me, he was able to motivate me to play the drums.

Recalling those years of drum training, I realize that they were fun. However, I believe that playing the drums was not as meaningful as experiencing other music, because there were no song lyrics involved. Personally, the voice of the performer is what my ear concentrates on when listening to music. Drums are only a part of the overall effect when the vocals make the song. This is probably why I feel so moved by Elvis and The Rolling Stones: their voices express dynamic personalities which seem to be able to influence me. I guess every performer intends to be influential.

I remember the first time I experienced what my effect on an audience. In high school, I inadvertently got involved in the spring musical productions. I was in my freshman year when the director asked me to be part of a dance. He explained he needed someone with the physical strength to lift course girls. The following year I figured I would addition for another course part. Surprisingly, I won a main supporting role in the 1950s musical Guys and Dolls. The positive response I received from the part, Nicely, Nicely, Johnson, and especially for my comical solo, amazed me. The next years I received larger parts and worked harder at improving my vocal and characterizations. No wonder the entertainers I like seem so energetic. They enjoy shining on stage.

While contemplating my own encounters with music, I cannot help but think how much music is a part of our lives. Daily in Los Angeles, thousands turn on the car radios while they endure crowded freeways. Even if they primary seek the traffic report or the news update, they eventually hear some music too. Playing music while people are in the shower, at work, or relaxing at home is natural. Besides daily routines, music also has a major role in many ceremonies. A graduation ceremony would lose some of its meaning if "Pomp and Circumstance" was not playing. The playing of deep sounding cords on the organ adds to the sorrowful moments during a funeral. If the organist does not perform "Here Comes the Bride," a wedding does not seem to properly begin.

Sporting events are not necessarily ceremonies, although for some they most certainly are. Even they are enhanced by music. When the USC Trojan Marching Band, The Spirit of Troy, performs "Conquest" or "Fight On," the intensity of the game rises. A baseball stadium organist prompts the fans to sign "Take Me Out to The Ballgame." Any hockey arena organist hopes his music will warrant rhythmic and handclapping.

Composing this story allowed me to discover my musical tastes includes comparing songs content with my life's content. Quite possibly, every individual looks for a different type of energy in music. The world continues contains millions of different songs and performances to satisfy one's desires. Hopefully, music has some meaning in everyone's life. Needless to say, it certainly has meaning in mine. I must agree with the lyrics: "It's only rock 'n' roll, but I like it."

Postscript: I finally saw Paul McCartney (one of my top favorite performers) at Dodger Stadium with my friend, Wally Gerlach, on Saturday, July 13, 2019. Sir Paul was spot on and exceeded my expectations.

I saw the Rolling Stones rock the Rose Bowl on Thursday, Aug. 22, 2019 with my friends, Jim Duffy and Dave Mitchell.

Your Life's Takeaways:

Who are your current musical influences? ____.

Who inspired your musical preferences? ____.

Who supported your musical talents and encouraged you to sing, write lyrics, or play an instrument?

List a song (s) that makes you think about a sad moment in your life. ____.

When no one is around, what song (s) do you enthusiastically sign outload? ____.

What song (s) provides a "musical track" to a fun and unforgettable time in your life? ____.

Chapter 16: Maintain Steadfast Awareness and Realize Your Life's Takeaways

Salutation Bishop Amat Memorial High School
La Puente, California
Graduation Day: June 1, 1980
Matthew Edmund Airey

Today, we celebrate the commencement of our graduating class of 1980.

Due to the completion of our four-year role in the Amat Family, we have individually reached a definite awareness in our lives.

You parents have now become aware that the child you once carried in your arms has suffered and matured through these past years. As a result of these experiences, they have learned the value of facing the challenges of life.

You faculty members have become aware that the students you have encountered have successfully been taught goodness, discipline, and science.

And we as students have become aware that together we have shared the joy and happiness of knowing and caring for one another. We have also become aware that it is difficult to compensate for the loss of a dear classmate and a beloved coach.

On such a memorable occasion, it is only proper that we join together in praise and thank Our Heavenly Father, who carried us through our Amat years.

Dear Lord,

We reflect on the triumphant memories of yesterday, and we thank you for our faith that has been nourished by Your continuous presence in our school.

We celebrate the accomplishments we have successfully achieve during our Amat years.

Lord, make us an enlightened example of Your Hope in the dark world of today.

We wish for many beautiful tomorrows like the ones we have experienced in the years' past.

But above all, we thank You for the Love that You have generously given us.

We beg You, Lord, that by the example of the Amat family, we continue to love.

To love when we feel like giving up.

To love when it hurts.

To love when it makes a difference.

And to love You forever. Amen.

Reflection: I have not read the content of this salutation since I wrote it 40 years ago. My dear mother continues to talk to me and guide me, because she was the one who placed copies of these potent and captivating words into a small box within a group of larger boxes stored in my garage. I recently went on a quest to go through and review these boxes with stored treasures.

I cannot describe the euphoria I felt holding the paper that represented feelings and emotions from four decades ago. Side note: I was able to discover other key writings, notes, cards, and mementoes during my review of boxes, except for the eulogy I delivered for my Papa Ed in 1992. I remain hopeful; however, it may have to be a sentimental document (I think that I wrote the eulogy on a legal pad versus on typewriter paper or via computer) that I commit simply to my emotional memory.

While I held this paper in my hands, I serenely closed my eyes to reflect on how I came up with the content. I affectionately recalled feeling that I had to come up with a simple theme, a word, to be good, be brief, and be gone. My dad used to advise this approach.

I told my parents one afternoon in our front living room, the theme, the word was awareness. We celebrated the four years of high school life, but I felt we needed to truly appreciate the current moment and be selflessly thankful for the present moment.

Steadfast Awareness. Number one. A classmate died a few weeks before our graduation. I am not going to share the circumstances, but what I remember most was how a few close friends of this person demonstrated such strength, poise, faith, and resiliency in honoring their friend. What a tragedy, what pain for the parents and the family surrounded by commencement celebrations. I was humbled and honored to be their classmate, maybe not a close classmate, but among their grace. Never again in our lives would we all be at the same place at the same time.

Steadfast Awareness. An unexpected passing of a legendary and beloved football coach and counselor, Tate Duff. Duff's simple encouragement to me during my freshmen counseling session with him challenged me. Coach allowed me to see potential accomplishments, I couldn't dream of as a young lad of 14-years-old. Coach told me if I continued my high-grade point average, I could receive the football scholar athlete award. And I eventually did. I know he did the same for thousands of others in his lifetime. Thank you, coach.

Steadfast Awareness. Our Parents' awareness of their sacrifices for their children, and hopefully, their children's awareness to truly appreciate their parental love. In 2019, a caring classmate shared with me what I had referenced in this salutation and within another 2010 class reunion prayer allowed her to recognize all of the sustenance and patronage she received from her benevolent parents. Holy Ned! Her sweet comment made me feel gratified.

Life's Takeaways: I was pleasantly surprised that I was able to concisely summarize these laudable goals in my formidable state:

> To love when we feel like giving up.
>
> To love when it hurts.
>
> To love when it makes a difference.

Final Note: June 1, 1980 was the 55th wedding anniversary of my grandparents, Ed and Helene Airey (Papa and Mama), who attended my graduation. I remember we celebrated their anniversary earlier that day at Mass and with a restaurant breakfast meal (my favorite meal at Michael J's Restaurant near The Donut Hole).

Your Life's Takeaways:

At this moment, how do you Maintain Steadfast Awareness in your life? ____.

Realize and write down Your Life's Takeaways. ____.

Appendix A: In Loving Memory of Edmund Francis Airey, Jr. June 27, 1928 – November 4, 2001.

Monday, November 12, 2001 – Veterans' Day
Saint Denis Catholic Church, Diamond Bar, California

In Ed's honor, the Airey family graciously welcomes donations to the following tax-deductible charities:

Bishop Amat High School
Ed Airey, Jr., Scholarship Fund
Msgr. Cremins Choral Room
14301 Fairgrove Avenue
La Puente, CA 91746
(626) 962-2495

Catholic Charities of Los Angeles, Inc.
James M. Wood Boulevard
PO Box 15095
Los Angeles, CA 90015-0095
(213)251-3400

PALLBEARERS:

Jean Airey, Brother

Joe Airey, Brother

Fred Ballew, Brother-In-Law

Eli De La Hoz, Brother-In-Law

Ralph Larsen, Brother-In-Law

George Gerberick, Brother-In-Law

HONORARY PALLBEARERS

Bishop Juan Arzube, seminarian friend

John Centeno, seminarian friend

James Duffy III, family friend

James Duffy IV, family friend

Don Engh, brother-in-law

Lefty Fontenrose, former co-worker

Joe Huarte, friend

Dave Kallgren, Amat parent, Confirmation Candidate

Charles Lanathoua, friend

Arnie Maldonado, former co-worker

Roger Nedry, former co-worker

Bob Webster, seminarian friend

"Reputations last longer than lives, and fortune favors the brave." Irish verse.

Mother Teresa's DO IT ANYWAY

People are often unreasonable, illogical and self-centered;
Forgive them anyway.

If you are kind, people may accuse you of selfish, ulterior motives;
Be kind anyway.

If you are successful, you will win some false friends and some true enemies;
Succeed anyway.

If you are honest and frank, people may cheat you;
Be honest and frank anyway.

What you spend years building, someone could destroy overnight;
Build anyway.

If you find serenity and happiness, they may be jealous;
Be happy anyway.

The good you do today, people will often forget tomorrow;
Do good anyway.

Give the world the best you have, and it may never be enough;
Give the world the best you've got anyway.

You see, in the final analysis, it is between you and your God;
It was never between you and them anyway.

Appendix B: In Loving Memory of Marguerite June Airey.
June 4, 1933 – January 6, 2020

Saturday, January 18, 2020
St. Elizabeth Ann Seton Church, Rowland Heights, California

Acknowledgments

Our hearts overflow with gratitude for the many loving souls who brightened Mrs. Marguerite's daily life and uplifted her through this celebration.

Caregiving:

Angelic Ramirez (lead caregiver); Cindi Barrera, Sandra Cisneros, Sylvia Cisneros, Ana Henriques, Lupe Mincitar.

Eucharistic Ministry:

Jack & Rose Ruehlman (St. Denis Catholic Community)

Celebration of Life:

Michael Engh, SJ & Linda Dumont (liturgy); David Caro (music); Teresa Waltrip (flowers & centerpieces); Amanda Santos, Audine Santos & Teresa Waltrip (memory table); Monica Froeber, Jodi McDaniel & Alison Wallis (photo collage & program)

Pallbearers

Connor James Airey (grandson)

Garrett Matthew Airey (grandson)

Shane Abbott Airey (grandson)

George S. Gerberick (brother)

Chuck Jensen (cousin)

Jim Waltrip (nephew-in-law)

Honorary Pallbearers

Christy Airey (daughter-in-law)

Kathy Airey (sister-in-law)

Lee Alfano (lifelong friend, Confirmation sponsor, maid-of-honor)

Skip Allen (cousin)

Hank Arellano (friend)

Nancy Armbrust (cousin)

Fred Ballew (brother-in-law)

Patty Ballew (sister-in-law)

Michael Collins (Gina's "Everlovin'", nicknamed by Marguerite)

Mary Lou De La Hoz (sister-in-law)

James Duffy IV (friend)

Don Engh (brother-in-law)

Marie Therese Engh (sister-in-law)

Adrienne Larsen (sister-in-law)

Ralph Larsen (brother-in-law)

Paulette Lee (cousin)

Jodi McDaniel (friend)

Robert Maywood, MD (friend)

Donation Suggestions in Her Honor

"Miss no single opportunity of making some small sacrifice, here by a smiling look, there by a kindly word; always doing the smallest right and doing it all for love." – St. Therese of Lisieux

Bishop Amat Memorial High School, Msgr. Cremins Choral Room:
https://www.bishopamat.org/apps/pages/index.jsp?uREC_ID=1156443&type=d&pREC_ID=1657771
Or: Attn. Steve Hagerty, 14301 Fairgrove Ave, La Puente, CA 91746
With Mom's encouragement both Matt and Gina participated in performing arts at our alma mater where Monsignor
Cremins was an inspiring chaplain, mentor, teacher, and friend.

Brady Campaign to Prevent Gun Violence:
https://www.bradyunited.org/donate/tax
Every day, 100 people in America are killed by gun violence. While Mom was usually mild-mannered, this senseless loss of life sparked her to pound her fist, literally, and become a loyal donor.

La Leche League International:

https://www.llli.org/donate/

When Mom was first pregnant in 1961, she was committed to breastfeed, but her doctor was not helpful. She educated herself through La Leche. Now we know the immense contribution of breastfeeding to healthy development of baby and mother.

Appendix C: In Memory of US Navy Commander William Joseph "Bill" Gault. 1954 - 2019

Bill's Funeral Mass held on Tuesday, March 19, 2019 at 10 AM at Saint Mary Magdalene, 1945 Illion Street, San Diego, CA 92110

Bill is buried at Miramar National Cemetery, 5795 Nobel Drive, San Diego, CA 92122.

<u>First Reading at the Funeral Mass read by Matt Airey.</u>
Isaiah 25:6a, 7-9
He will destroy death forever.
A reading from the Book of the Prophet Isaiah

On this mountain the LORD of hosts
    will provide for all peoples.
On this mountain he will destroy
    the veil that veils all peoples,
The web that is woven over all nations;
    he will destroy death forever.
The Lord GOD will wipe away
    the tears from all faces;
The reproach of his people he will remove
    from the whole earth; for the LORD has spoken.

On that day it will be said:

"Behold our God, to whom we looked to save us!

This is the LORD for whom we looked;

let us rejoice and be glad that he has saved us!"

The word of the Lord.

Matt Airey's Post.

"If you're not gonna go ALL the way, why go at ALL?"- Broadway Joe Willie Namath, New York Jets.

My dear brother Bill. Thank you for your love, laughter and friendship. I love you. I cherish the memories. Fight On!

Denise. Billy. God's Speed.